"Bloom shows you with powerful clarity how to weave gospel-priorities through all your work and all your moments."

Ann Voskamp, author, *New York Times* bestseller, *One Thousand Gifts*

"Jon Bloom has an extraordinary gift for mining rare gems hidden in familiar Bible stories and characters. His insights are imaginative, biblical, and practical. Jon prompts readers to see with new eyes, examine their hearts, and face life's challenges with renewed perspective and joy. I enthusiastically recommend *Things Not Seen!*"

Randy Alcorn, Founder and Director, Eternal Perspectives Ministries; author, *Heaven*, *If God Is Good*, and *Money, Possessions & Eternity*

"I trust a writer who not only sees deeply into the treasures of Scripture, but takes what he sees into his soul, and with it serves his family, church, and friends. Jon Bloom is one of those writers. And one of my treasures is to be one of those friends. We welcome you into this circle of joy."

John Piper, Founder, desiringGod.org; Chancellor, Bethlehem College and Seminary

"Jon Bloom unpacks the deepest truths about God in a way that every human can receive. You don't want to miss anything he writes—this book is no exception. Prepare for your faith to expand."

Jennie Allen, author, *Restless*; Founder and CEO, IF:Gathering

"The Bible is full of stories not just so we have something to read to our children at night, but to help us understand what it is like to walk with God in a broken world. Jon Boom revives the age-old tradition of using biblically informed fictional additions to creatively retell the Bible's most familiar stories. He also intersperses pastoral insights as a skilled soul physician. This book will stir and encourage your faith."

Adrian Warnock, author, *Hope Reborn* and *Raised with Christ*

TRUTH FOR LIFE®

THE BIBLE-TEACHING MINISTRY OF **ALISTAIR BEGG**

The mission of Truth For Life is to teach the Bible with clarity and relevance so that unbelievers will be converted, believers will be established, and local churches will be strengthened.

Daily Program

Each day, Truth For Life distributes the Bible teaching of Alistair Begg across the U.S., and in several locations outside of the U.S. on over 1,700 radio outlets. To find a radio station near you, visit *truthforlife.org/station-finder.*

Free Teaching

The daily program, and Truth For Life's entire teaching archive of over 2,000 Bible-teaching messages, can be accessed for free online and through Truth For Life's full-feature mobile app. A daily app is also available that provides direct access to the daily message and daily devotional. Download the free mobile apps at *truthforlife.org/app* and listen free online at *truthforlife.org.*

At-Cost Resources

Books and full-length teaching from Alistair Begg on CD, DVD and MP3CD are available for purchase *at cost, with no mark up.* Visit *truthforlife.org/store.*

Where To Begin?

If you're new to Truth For Life and would like to know where to begin listening and learning, find starting point suggestions at *truthforlife.org/firststep.* For a full list of ways to connect with Truth For Life, visit *truthforlife.org/subscribe.*

Contact Truth For Life

P.O. Box 398000 Cleveland, Ohio 44139
phone 1 (888) 588-7884   **email** letters@truthforlife.org
 /truthforlife   @truthforlife   truthforlife.org

THINGS

NOT SEEN

THINGS

NOT SEEN

A FRESH LOOK AT OLD STORIES
OF TRUSTING GOD'S PROMISES

JON BLOOM

FOREWORD BY **ANN VOSKAMP**

CROSSWAY

WHEATON, ILLINOIS

Things Not Seen: A Fresh Look at Old Stories of Trusting God's Promises

Copyright © 2015 by Desiring God

Published by Crossway
    1300 Crescent Street
    Wheaton, Illinois 60187

Cover design & photography: Josh Dennis

First printing 2015

Printed in the United States of America

Trade paperback ISBN: 978-1-4335-4699-0
ePub ISBN: 978-1-4335-4702-7
PDF ISBN: 978-1-4335-4700-3
Mobipocket ISBN: 978-1-4335-4701-0

Library of Congress Cataloging-in-Publication Data

Bloom, Jon, 1965–
 Things not seen : a fresh look at old stories of trusting
God's promises / Jon Bloom ; foreword by Ann Voskamp.
  pages cm
 Includes bibliographical references and index.
 ISBN 978-1-4335-4699-0 (tp)
 1. Bible stories. 2. Bible—Criticism, interpretation, etc.
3. Bible—Biography. I. Title.
BS546.B56   2015
242'.5—dc23   2014030574

| VP | | | 25 | 24 | 23 | 22 | 21 | 20 | 19 | 18 | 17 | 16 | 15 |
| 15 | 14 | 13 | 12 | 11 | 10 | 9 | 8 | 7 | 6 | 5 | 4 | 3 | 2 | 1 |

To Levi, Eliana, Peter, Moriah, and Micah

You are my beloved children; with you
I am well pleased. (Luke 3:2)

You have taught me more about trusting the
promises of God than you may ever know.

CONTENTS

FOREWORD

ANN VOSKAMP

I HEARD ONCE OF a man who split black ash and wove baskets.

And he wove prayer through every basket.

The man wore faded plaid and old denim and lived alone high up in the Appalachians where the dirt didn't grow crops, but it could grow basket trees.

He lived such a distance up in the hills that he really didn't think the cost of transportation to some Saturday morning market would exceed any profits from selling his baskets. Nevertheless, each day he cut trees and sawed them into logs and then pounded the logs with a mallet, to free all the splint ribbons from those trees. Splint slapped the floor.

And the basket-making man, he simply worked unhurried and unseen by the world, his eyes and heart fixed on things unseen.

"When the heart is at rest in Jesus—unseen, unheard by the world—the Spirit comes, and softly fills the believing soul, quickening all, renewing all within," writes Robert Murray M'Cheyne.[1]

Day after day, the man cut ash, pulled splint, stacked baskets. He said that as he held the damp splint and he braided— under and over, under and over—that God was simply teaching him to weave prayers into every basket, to fill the empty baskets, all the emptiness, with eternal, unseen things.

---

[1] Andrew Bonar, *Memoir and Remains of the Rev. Robert Murray M'Cheyne* (London: Hamilton, Adams, and Co., 1845), 461.

It was like under all the branches of those basket-growing trees, he knew what that clergyman James H. Aughey wrote: "As a weak limb grows stronger by exercise, so will your faith be strengthened by the very efforts you make in stretching it out toward things unseen."[2]

Come the end of the year, after long months of bending over baskets, bending in prayer, when his stacks of baskets threatened to topple over, the man kneeled down under those trees that grew baskets—and lit those baskets with a match.

The flames devoured and rose higher and cackled long into the night.

Then, come morning, when the heat died away, satiated, the basket-making man stood long in the quiet. He watched how the wind blew away the ashes of all his work.

To the naked eye, it would appear that the man had nothing to show for the work. All the product of his hands was made papery ash—*but his prayers had survived fire.*

The prayers we weave into the matching of the socks, the working of our hands, the toiling of the hours, they survive fire.

It's the things unseen that survive fire.

Love. Relationship. Worship. Prayer. Communion.

All Things Unseen—and Centered in Christ.

It doesn't matter so much what we leave unaccomplished—*but that our priority was things unseen.*

Again, today, that's always the call: slay the idol of the seen. Slay the idol of focusing on only what can be seen, lauded, noticed. Today, a thousand times again today, I will preach

---

[2]John H. Aughey, *Spiritual Gems of the Ages* (Cincinnati: Elm Street Printing, 1886), 95.

His truth to this soul prone to wander, that wants nothing more than the gracious smile of our Father: *"Unseen. Things Unseen. Invest in Things Unseen. The Unexpected Priority is always Things Unseen."*

"Pray to your Father, who is unseen. Then your Father, who sees what is done in secret . . ." (Matt. 6:6 NIV).

"For the things that are seen are transient, but the things that are unseen are eternal" (2 Cor. 4:18).

It's the things unseen that are the most important things.

Though the seen product of the baskets may have gone up in a flame of smoke, it was the unseen prayers that rose up like incense that had changed the man, much like Thomas Carlyle said: "It is the unseen and the spiritual in people, that determines the outward and the actual."[3]

When the heart and mind focus on things *unseen*, that's when there's a *visible change* in *us*.

The outward and the visible only become like Christ to the extent we focus on the unseen and invisible *person of Christ*.

"In truth, the ideas and images in men's minds are the invisible powers that constantly govern them," writes Jonathan Edwards.[4]

These pages you hold in your hand, these are a rare and unforgettable focusing. After meeting Jon Bloom, you walk away quietly saying: "He is so much like Jesus." And when you walk away from these pages—that is exactly what will happen: you will have become so much like Jesus.

---

[3] Thomas Carlyle, *The People's Edition of Thomas Carlyle's Works*, 37 vols., *Wanting* (London: Chapman and Hall, 1888), 3.

[4] Jonathan Edwards, *The Works of Jonathan Edwards*, vol. 1, *Freedom of the Will*, ed. Paul Ramsey (New Haven, CT: Yale University Press, 1957), 218.

The ideas and images and truths that Jon Bloom memorably guides into the recesses of the mind and heart, usher in the invisible power of Christ to govern the worries and lies and anxieties and stresses—and make them obedient to his sovereign will and relentless love and perfect ways. Jon Bloom is the wisest of guides, the most tender of pastors, the most honest of truth-tellers, and the most skillful of theologians—who shows you with powerful clarity how to weave gospel-priorities through all your work, all your moments: *Things Not Seen, Priorities Things Not Seen.*

Turn these profound pages and you will know it: your heart and mind focusing on his invisible kingdom.

Then go ahead—

Weave your baskets—

and the invisible kingdom will be made blazingly visible in our midst.

Ann Voskamp
author of the *New York Times* bestsellers,
One Thousand Gifts: A Dare to Live Fully Right Where You Are
and *The Greatest Gift*

the farm, Ontario, Canada,
December 1, 2014

A WORD TO
THE READER

HEBREWS 11 IS IN the Bible to remind us that God hides his most precious treasures for his saints in their most difficult and painful experiences.

Think of how Abraham and Sarah agonized over their infertility for twenty-five years before God fulfilled his promise of Isaac. Think of how Isaac and Rebekah agonized over the treacherous and nearly murderous rivalry between Jacob and Esau. Think of how Jacob agonized for years in grief over the belief that wild beasts had killed Joseph. Think of how Moses agonized for forty years in the Midian wilderness over his lost opportunity to deliver his enslaved people, and then struggled another forty years in the Sinai wilderness over his people's faithlessness. Think of how David agonized for years as Saul hunted him like an animal.

Now think of the blessing that each agony eventually produced.

This motif, of agony giving birth to glorious blessing, climaxed in Jesus's unparalleled agony on the cross and in the disciples' agony over the loss of their messianic rabbi, only to unleash the greatest blessing the world has ever known when Jesus was raised from the dead.

And the motif has continued since the time of Christ. Saints throughout church history have agonized through difficult labors, imprisonments, terrible persecutions; danger from robbers, unbelievers, false brothers, travel hazards, natural disasters, hunger, cold, and exposure; the sorrows of disease, disability, family strife; and on top of those, "the daily pressure . . . of . . . anxiety for all the churches" (see 2 Cor. 11:23–28).

Now think of the blessings the agonies of the church age have yielded.

Hebrews 11 reminds us that God is doing far more than we can see in our agonies—these things that are so painful at times that they seem unbearable. We plead for God to deliver us from them, and we wonder why he keeps letting them go on.

The purpose of this book, like Hebrews 11, is to remind us that we are in good company when we feel bewildered by the struggle. It seeks to imaginatively draw us into very real people's very real experiences of walking by faith, not by sight (2 Cor. 5:7), and to allow our brothers and sisters from history who are now in the great cloud of witnesses to encourage us to hold on and to not give up (Heb. 12:1). They remind us to trust God's promises more than our perceptions. For faith is "the conviction of things not seen" (Heb. 11:1). Promises will hold us up when perceptions make us sink.

We do well to listen to these precious biblical friends who have run the race before us. Their example reminds us not to begrudge the difficult afflictions we endure, because they are producing for us "an eternal weight of glory beyond all comparison" (2 Cor. 4:17). Their stories remind us that God hides his most precious treasures in our most difficult and painful experiences.

Jon Bloom
Minneapolis, MN

GRATITUDE

I OWE MY FIVE children, Levi, Eliana, Peter, Moriah, and Micah, more that I can possibly express. God has used them and continues to use them more than they know to teach me to lean hard on his promises and not to trust in my frail and often mistaken understanding. I thank God every morning for the gifts of their precious lives and pray that somehow, through his strange and wonderful ways, God will impart grace to them through their stumbling and often deficient father. I dedicate this book to them with the prayer that it may become one of those ways.

I simply can't thank God enough for my priceless wife Pam, who joyfully and prayerfully carried more than her share of our life load as I wrote (especially as the deadlines loomed). Profound thanks to Ann Voskamp, who somehow carved time out of her incredibly full life to read this book and write a stunning and very gracious foreword. Special thanks also to John Piper, whose influence on me is pervasive. And to David Mathis, Jonathan Parnell, Bryan DeWire, and Joseph Scheumann, who improved various initial story drafts. I'm so thankful for Karalee Reinke, who carefully combed through the early manuscript and significantly improved this book. And it is a joy to thank the amazing team at Crossway: Justin Taylor, Josh Dennis, Amy Kruis, Janni Firestone, Angie Cheatham, Matt Tully, and my gracious editor, Tara Davis. What a privilege it is to work with you.

I'm deeply grateful to my colleagues at Desiring God, Scott Anderson and Josh Etter, for the patience and encouragement they extended to me during the months it took to complete this project. And to Matthew Soderholm, who passed away during the final stage of writing. I miss your gentle spirit and your gracious wisdom, Matt. Thank you for working so hard and so well for this mission.

Jesus, my deepest thanks is always reserved for you. You have always been faithful to your word, though I have not always been faithful to trust it. Thank you for the amazing grace you have extended to me. Thank you for hiding your most precious treasures in the most difficult and painful experiences. And thank you for all that you have done to teach me to walk by faith (2 Cor. 5:7) and put my greatest trust in things not seen (Heb. 11:1). I look forward to the day when the dim mirror of this age is removed and I finally get to see you face to face (1 Cor. 13:12). I know you long for that day, too (John 17:24). May it be soon.

And [Joseph's brothers] drew Joseph up and lifted him out of the pit, and sold him to the Ishmaelites for twenty shekels of silver. They took Joseph to Egypt.

GENESIS 37:28

"God sent me before you to preserve for you a remnant on earth, and to keep alive for you many survivors. So it was not you who sent me here, but God."

GENESIS 45:7-8

1

YOUR SIN IS NO MATCH FOR GOD'S GRACE

JOSEPH'S BROTHERS AND GRACE

Based mainly on Genesis 45

THE OLD HYMN SAYS it beautifully: "Grace, grace, God's grace; grace that is greater than all my sin."[1]

But the grace of God is not only great enough to "pardon and cleanse within." It is so powerful, as Joseph's older brothers learned in Genesis 45, that it can take the most horrible sin that you have ever committed against another, or that has ever been committed against you, and make it the slave of God's mercy.

∞

"What do you mean he's *alive*?" Jacob had no place to put Reuben's words.

"I know it's unbelievable, Father," Reuben replied. "We hardly believe it, and we saw him with our own eyes. The Egyptian lord—the one who demanded that we bring Benjamin—he is Joseph. He's not only alive, he's . . ." Reuben stumbled over the strange sentence. "He's now ruling Egypt for Pharaoh."

---

[1] "Grace Greater Than Our Sin," Julia H. Johnston, 1911.

Jacob squinted skeptically. A son dead for two decades is not easily resurrected. "You are cruel to tell me such a thing unless you have no doubt."

"I have no doubt, Father. It's going to take hours to tell you everything. But we spoke with him. We ate with him in his house."

Simeon couldn't resist: "He sat us around the table in the order of our births! Before any of us knew who he was! We thought he was a magician."

"And you should have seen how much food he placed before Benjamin!" joked Zebulun, giving Benjamin's head an affectionate push.

Reuben continued, "He told us himself, Father: 'I am your brother, Joseph.' We responded just like you are now. I thought he was tricking us. But after talking to him for hours, there's no doubt. It's him. And the first thing he wanted to know was, 'Is my father still alive?'" (Gen 45:3).

Jacob's stony expression didn't change, though his eyes overflowed. He moved them from son to son, lingering on Benjamin, and returning to Reuben. "But you showed me his bloody robe. He was attacked by a wild animal. If he survived, why didn't he ever come home? Why would he go to Egypt? Joseph would never have forsaken me."

The moment had come—the one they had dreaded the whole way home. For twenty-two years they had kept this festering wound of wickedness concealed from their father. But now God had exposed it. Shame bent the heads of nine sons. Judah was the exception. He had asked to break this news to their father. He had led in their sin. He would lead in owning it.

"Joseph didn't forsake you, Father," said Judah, stepping forward. "*He* was forsaken. No, worse, he was betrayed."

Jacob stared at Judah. "Betrayed by whom?"

Judah pushed hard the heavy words. "By his own brothers.

Brothers who hated him for having his father's favor. Brothers who hated him for having God's favor. In all honesty, we actually talked of killing him, but decided instead to profit from his demise. We sold him to Ishmaelite traders who were on their way to Egypt. To my lasting and terrible shame, Father, that was my idea—to sell my own brother as a slave. The blood on his robe was goat's blood. We were the wild animals."

Jacob sat down. Anger and hope churned together in his soul. The silence was long.

Judah broke it by saying softly, "His dream came true." Jacob looked up again. "Joseph's dream: it came true," continued Judah. "All eleven of us bowed down before him in Egypt. We sold him into slavery because of his dream of ruling over us, never dreaming as we did it that we were helping bring it to pass."

Reuben added, "Joseph holds no bitterness, Father. You know what he told us? 'God sent me before you to preserve for you a remnant on earth, and to keep alive for you many survivors. So it was not you who sent me here, but God'" (Gen. 45:7–8).

"In fact," said Judah, "he wants us all to come live near him in Egypt to escape the famine. That's why we've brought all these wagons. He said, 'You must tell my father of all my honor in Egypt, and of all that you have seen. Hurry and bring my father down here'" (Gen. 45:13).

Jacob thought quietly for a long time. Then he shook his head and said, "It is enough; Joseph my son is still alive. I will go and see him before I die" (Gen. 45:28).

○ ○

What Joseph's ten older brothers did to him was heinous. They made him the merchandise of international human trafficking. They subjected him to slavery and sexual abuse. They effectively threw him, with no rights or defense, into prison to rot.

But note Joseph's words: "It was not you who sent me here, but God" (Gen. 45:8). Neither treacherous siblings nor a woman's lust nor the shame of prison nor a cupbearer's neglect could thwart the purpose of God (Job 42:2) in preserving God's people (Gen. 45:7) and fulfilling God's promise (Gen. 15:13). God made evil the slave of his grace.

And he's doing the same for you. God is doing more good than you can imagine through the most painful experiences of your life.

If you've sinned against someone, do everything in your power to make things right. But know this: your sin is no match for God's grace.

And if you're facing the consequences of another's sin, take heart. Stay faithful. God knows, and he knows what he's doing. In time, you will see God turn what man means for evil into the slave of God's mercy.

"The one who has the bride is the bridegroom. The friend of the bridegroom, who stands and hears him, rejoices greatly at the bridegroom's voice. Therefore this joy of mine is now complete. He must increase, but I must decrease."

JOHN 3:29-30

2

"HE MUST INCREASE, BUT I MUST DECREASE"

JOHN THE BAPTIST AND HUMILITY

Based on John 3:25–30

WE ALL WANT TO finish well, but so many of us do not. Why? Because we too easily cherish our roles in the Great Wedding more than the Wedding itself. This is why John the Baptist must become our mentor.

○ ○

It was all a bit hard to comprehend.

John's disciples understood his mission. John was preparing the way for the Hope of Israel. The long-expected time was so close, and the anticipation was thrilling. And on that climactic day when Jesus appeared and John publicly proclaimed him the Messiah—the wonder could yield no words.

Yes, John's disciples understood his mission, but they hadn't expected to feel sidelined by it.

For the past year John had blazed across Judea like a shooting star, the first real prophet in Israel for four centuries. All eyes, from king to peasant, had been on him, and he called them all to account, including the self-righteous Pharisees. When John spoke, God moved, and people repented and were baptized. No one spoke like this man. From all over Palestine, people flocked to hear him. The oppressed, weary people of God, living under Tiberius's thumb and Antipas's corruption, had hope again.

John's disciples had been right in the middle of this remarkable move of God. Then, abruptly, they weren't. The surge moved past them toward Jesus. Of course, it was wrong to be envious of the Messiah. But still, how could their beloved rabbi—and they with him—suddenly be relegated to the periphery, after all that God had done through them?

They couldn't help but express their perplexity to John: "Rabbi, he who was with you across the Jordan, to whom you bore witness—look, he is baptizing, and all are going to him" (John 3:26).

John, who had been staring at the water, looked up at them. His intense eyes were filled with joy.

John said nothing for a moment. He felt compassion for them. He understood. He knew their inner conflict. He knew their sincere godly ambition for the kingdom. And he knew their selfish ambition to have prominent roles in it. He knew how the latter insidiously wove itself into the fabric of the former and how difficult it could be to discern one from the other. This was a moment of unraveling for them, of heart exposure.

John had spent a lifetime being prepared for his brief ministry of introduction. During his years in the wilderness, God ruthlessly exposed his deeply entrenched and multifaceted pride, and trained John to die to it. This discipline had brought about the peaceful fruit of the righteousness of faith. John learned to anticipate his replacement more than his own role. He learned to love the Bridegroom's appearing and not love the celebrity of being the Bridegroom's best man. But that shift in affection had not come easily.

Learning to love the Great Wedding more than their part

in it would not come easily to John's disciples either. He knew they loved the Bridegroom, but their hearts required further recalibration. When the blessed Lord grants one a role to play, one must perform it faithfully, but never grasp it. The role is not the reward. The Lord is the reward.

With affectionate empathy, John replied, "A person cannot receive even one thing unless it is given him from heaven." He waved them to sit down beside him. "You yourselves bear me witness, that I said, 'I am not the Christ,' but have been sent before him. The one who has the bride is the bridegroom. The friend of the bridegroom, who stands and hears him, rejoices greatly at the bridegroom's voice. Therefore this joy of mine is now complete. He must increase, but I must decrease" (John 3:27–29).

○ ○

Our role is not our reward, Jesus is. Roles will begin and they will end. The only way for us to end well is to have our hearts recalibrated. Jesus must increase and we must decrease.

What rises in your heart at the thought of Jesus giving another person a more prominent role in his Wedding? How much do you long to have a more prominent role? How well are you prepared to let go of the role he has given you? What if he gives another your role?

In our individual and temporary earthly roles, the Wedding is not about us. It's about Jesus and his bride. And we should never compete with the Bridegroom for the bride's attention and affection.

Then he said, "Let me go, for the day has broken." But Jacob said, "I will not let you go unless you bless me."

GENESIS 32:26

3

"I WILL NOT LET YOU GO UNLESS YOU BLESS ME"

JACOB AND WRESTLING WITH GOD

Based on Genesis 32

IS THERE A FEAR staring you in the face right now? Are you shaking in your faith in God's promises? Are you praying desperately for God's help? Do not doubt; God will answer you. But you might, like Jacob in Genesis 32, be surprised by his answer.

○ ○

Jacob leaned on his staff, staring at the stars. He was looking for hope. "Number the stars, if you are able to number them. . . . So shall your offspring be" (Gen. 15:5). Yahweh had promised this to Father Abraham.

Jacob's body was tired, but his mind was restless. Daylight was approaching, and Esau with it.

He wrapped himself tighter in his cloak and squatted down. He was cold, and the fire had cooled to glowing coals. He stared at the ground. "Your offspring shall be like the dust of the earth" (Gen. 28:14). Yahweh had revealed this promise to him two decades ago, when all he carried to Haran was this staff.

Now he was returning home with eleven sons and a daughter, a God-blessed abundance of offspring, even if not yet as the dust of the earth.

But Esau was coming. And four hundred men were with him. Hadn't the fire of revenge cooled after twenty years? Four hundred men! This was more than enough to turn his beloved children into the dust of the earth.

Jacob prayed desperately. "O God of my father Abraham, God of my father Isaac, deliver me from Esau! You commanded me, 'Return to the land of your fathers and to your kindred.' And you promised, 'I will be with you' [see Gen. 31:3]. Yahweh! Four hundred men will wipe us out! Please! I need you with me!"

Just then, Jacob heard splashing. He looked up, squinting toward the Jabbok. A man was crossing the ford, heading in his direction. Jacob didn't recognize the determined gait. He stood. Fear shot through him. Esau? No. This wasn't Esau's stride. But he wasn't relieved. He knew this man was coming for him.

The stranger stopped three feet in front of Jacob. He looked strong. His eyes were intense and inscrutable. Neither man spoke. Jacob felt a familiar fear, but he couldn't place it. Had they met before?

Instinctively Jacob began to raise his staff in defense. With startling speed, the man wrenched it away and threw it aside. Jacob was more confused. What did he want? Then the stranger struck a stance every Semite boy would recognize. Wrestling was an ancient martial art, and this silent adversary wanted a contest. Jacob was perplexed, but knew he had no choice.

The men circled twice, eyeing each other. Then a twitch, an adrenaline rush, and the two locked in grappled combat. This nameless foe was powerful. Yet Jacob was surprised at his ability to counter him.

The longer they struggled, the more Jacob sensed that his

opponent was no mere man. He now placed the familiar fear: it was what he felt at every encounter with Yahweh. And he began to understand that this wrestling was somehow connected to all that lay ahead of him tomorrow. Who was this? An angel? Was it God? Was this struggle an answered prayer?

The men broke apart, each leaning on his knees to catch his breath. They shared a glance of recognition. And a desperate resolve formed in Jacob. As a deceiver living among deceivers, Jacob had learned that God was the only rock that could support his trust. And the only real source of his hope was God's promised blessing. His life depended on it, now more than ever. God was now within his grasp. Jacob would not let him leave without obtaining his blessing.

The stranger's attention suddenly turned to the horizon. Light was glowing over the eastern hills. Jacob saw his moment. Darting quickly, he seized his opponent from behind and locked his hands around his chest. The challenger tried to free himself, but Jacob held fast. The man swung his fist down on Jacob's right hip. Jacob screamed as the pain exploded. His leg gave way, but his grip did not. He could endure pain, but he could not endure this day without God's blessing.

For the first time, the man spoke: "Let me go, for the day has broken."[1] Wincing hard, Jacob whispered through clenched teeth, "I will not let you go unless you bless me." Instantly he felt the man yield. The contest was over. "What is your name?" the man asked. "Jacob," came a groan. "Your name shall no longer be called Jacob, but Israel, for you have striven with God and with men, and have prevailed."

Jacob crumpled to the ground and grabbed his hip. Striven with God? Panting, he said, "Please tell me your name." The man's eyes were intense with affection. He said, "Why is it that

---

[1] The quotations in this paragraph and the following are from Genesis 32:26–29.

you ask my name?" And with that he turned and crossed back over the Jabbok.

○ ○

Jacob began the night believing his greatest need was to escape from Esau. He ended the night believing his greatest need was to trust in the blessing of God's promise. What changed him from fearing man to trusting God's word was prolonged and painful wrestling with God.

Sometimes, in your battle with unbelief, your greatest ally will wrestle you—he might even make you limp—until you're desperate enough to say, "I will not let you go unless you bless me." It is a great mercy to be brought to the point where you're desperate enough to insist on what you need the most.

"And I tell you, make friends for yourselves by means of un-righteous wealth, so that when it fails they may receive you into the eternal dwellings."

LUKE 16:9

4

BE GENEROUS WITH YOUR MASTER'S MONEY

SIMON THE ZEALOT, MATTHEW, AND GENEROSITY

Shortly after Luke 16:1-9

JESUS ONCE TOLD HIS disciples an odd parable in which he used a dishonest manager to demonstrate that we should be shrewd with our money. What did he mean? Imagine his disciples Simon (the Zealot) and Matthew (the tax collector) discussing this parable.

○ ○

"Matthew, you know more about these things than I do. Why did the Master commend the dishonest manager's shrewdness?"

Simon's question stung a little, and Matthew's look said so.

"Oh. I didn't mean that the way it sounded," said an embarrassed Simon.

Simon and Matthew were unlikely friends now. They hadn't liked each other in the beginning.

Simon had been a zealot with a lethal hatred of the Romans. He had once sworn himself to the sacred cause of driving them out of Israel. But even more than the Romans, Simon loathed Jews who helped the emperor subjugate and pillage God's people. Jews like Matthew.

Matthew had collected taxes for Rome—and himself. He simply saw it as a shrewd and lucrative career move. Prior to Jesus calling him from his booth, Matthew had zero time for the idealism of foolish zealots like Simon. Theirs was a utopic delusion—a handful of angry Jews taking on Caesar's legions. They had a death wish, an appointment with a Roman cross.

Now the former zealot and former tax collector were fast friends. Only Jesus could have made that happen.

"What *did* you mean?" Matthew asked.

"I just meant . . . you used to be . . ."

"A shrewd, dishonest manager?"

"I'm not saying you were just like . . ."

"Stop tripping over yourself, Simon," said Matthew, laying aside the vestiges of his pride. "I was every bit as shrewdly dishonest, and worse. I know it. It's just painful to remember what I used to be. So which master are you saying commended the manager?"

"Well, that's where I'm confused," replied Simon. "It almost sounded like Jesus commended the self-protective actions of the manager. But I know that's not right. How is this corrupt scoundrel supposed to be an example for 'the sons of light'?"

Matthew smiled and said, "Generosity."

"Generosity?" said Simon incredulously. "The only thing he was generous with was his master's money!"

"Exactly. Simon, that's *our* Master's point. The manager used his master's money to win favor with those who could provide him a place to live when he lost his job."

"And that's supposed to be a good thing?" said Simon, confused.

"No, Jesus isn't saying the man's dishonesty was good. He's saying that as a 'son of this world,' the man knew how this world works. He used worldly shrewdness so he wouldn't be homeless, and even his worldly master appreciated his cunning. Jesus is saying that the 'sons of light' need to be at least as shrewd about how the kingdom works."

"Which is completely different," said Simon.

"Completely," agreed Matthew. "But what we do is similar to what the dishonest manager did."

"You mean we're generous with *our* Master's money."

"Right."

Simon thought for a moment. "So, in a sense it's another way of saying, 'Sell your possessions, and give to the needy' so that we will have 'a treasure in the heavens that does not fail' [Luke 12:33]. Shrewd 'sons of light' give away 'unrighteous wealth' and make friends of God, who is our 'eternal dwelling' [Deut. 33:27]."

"Exactly. That's the financial shrewdness *our* Master commends."

○ ○

Our heavenly Master has made us all managers of "unrighteous wealth" (Luke 16:9). As John Piper says,

> The possession of money in this world is a test run for eternity. Can you pass the test of faithfulness with your money? Do you use it as a means of proving the worth of God and the joy you have in supporting his cause? Or does the way you use it prove that what you really enjoy is things, not God?[1]

These are questions we all must ask ourselves, because Jesus wants us to be shrewd with our money (Luke 16:8–9). Kingdom shrewdness looks like this:

---

[1]John Piper, sermon, "Preparing to Receive Christ: Hearing Moses and the Prophets," desiringGod.com, December 14, 1986, http://www.desiringgod.org/sermons/preparing-to -receive-christ-hearing-moses-and-the-prophets.

Fear not, little flock, for it is your Father's good pleasure to give you the kingdom. Sell your possessions, and give to the needy. Provide yourselves with moneybags that do not grow old, with a treasure in the heavens that does not fail, where no thief approaches and no moth destroys. For where your treasure is, there will your heart be also. (Luke 12:32–34)

"I am not able to carry all this people alone. . . . If you will treat me like this, kill me at once."

NUMBERS 11:14-15

5

HARD, HEARTBREAKING, HOPEFUL SPIRITUAL LEADERSHIP

MOSES AND LEADERSHIP

Various Texts

ANY TIME A SELFISH sinner is tasked with leading other selfish sinners in a Godward direction—whether in families, friendships, small groups, churches, or broader movements—there's going to be trouble.

Take Moses, for example. No Old Testament leader was as meek (Num. 12:3), had more intimate interaction with God (Ex. 33:11), and faced more harsh and unjust criticism by those he led, as Moses.

Here's an overview of Moses's experience as a spiritual leader:

At first the Israelites rallied behind Moses (Ex. 4:31).
But when Pharaoh increased their work, they completely lost faith in him (5:21).

After the Passover, the people deeply revered Moses (Ex. 12:28).
But their trust quickly evaporated on the seashore when Pharaoh's army showed up (14:11).

When the sea opened for them and closed on the Egyptians, the people believed Moses was a great hero (Ex. 14:31).

That is, until they came to Marah and found bitter water (15:24).

But God sweetened the water and the people gave their grumbling a rest as they drank (Ex. 15:27).

Until they got hungry. Then Moses took a serious dive in the polls (16:2).

Then the manna fell, and they gathered as much as they could eat (Ex. 16:18).

Until they got thirsty again. Then they wanted to stone Moses (17:4).

In Exodus 18, the demand for Moses's counsel was growing overwhelming (v. 13).

Thank God for Jethro! (vv. 19–23)

Before Moses climbed Mount Sinai, the people pledged obedience to the Lord (Ex. 19:8).

But when Moses tarried on the mountain as he met with God, the people decided to elect a golden calf to lead them (chap. 32).

When they stood weeping at the doors of their tents because they were tired of eating boring old miracle manna, Moses cried out to God: "I am not able to carry all this people alone . . . If you will treat me like this, kill me at once" (Num. 11:14–15).

God mercifully gave Moses some elders and the people some meat (vv. 18–20).

To add heartbreak to insult, Miriam and Aaron publicly opposed Moses because of his interracial marriage (Numbers 12).

But God confirmed his servant Moses and humbled Miriam with leprosy for seven days (vv. 7–15).

When the twelve spies presented their Promised Land Report, the people threatened to depose Moses and Aaron and stone Joshua and Caleb (Num. 14:5–10).

Moses and Aaron fell on their faces, tore their clothes, and pleaded with the people to trust the Lord (vv. 5–7). But the people still grumbled, and forty years of lament followed.

Korah led a coup, and God wiped out the rebels in the Israelite camp.

But the people blamed . . . yep, Moses (Num. 16:41).

They got thirsty again at Meribah and again grumbled against Moses, who lost his temper and struck the rock.

God gave the people water, but barred Moses from Canaan (Num. 20:10–13).

One would think the lesson might have sunk in by now, but again the people complained against Moses about food and water (Num. 21:5).

God gave the people fiery serpents instead (v. 6).

And after all this, many Israelites rejected the Lord and embraced Baal (Numbers 25).

Sigh.

○ ○

Moses's experience reminds us that spiritual leadership is often hard and sometimes heartbreaking. It is accompanied with adversity and opposition. The Bible illustrates this over and over, culminating in the life of Jesus. A prophet may have honor, but not usually among those who know him best (Matt. 13:57).

So who in the world would want to be a Christian leader? Only a servant (Matt. 23:11) who walks in the faith-footsteps of the Great Servant-Leader (1 Pet. 2:21) will be willing to take up the call.

Here's what it means to be a Christlike servant-leader:

- Like Jesus, we don't hope in people's approval, we hope in God (John 2:24–25; Ps. 43:5).
- We are not defensive, but leave our vindication to God (Isa. 54:17).
- We, like Moses, faithfully teach and live by God's Word (Deut. 32:47).
- We don't hope in our own giftedness, but "in God who raises the dead" (2 Cor. 1:9).
- We believe that we are God's "workmanship, created in Christ Jesus for good works" (Eph. 2:10).
- We believe that God is always at work in our work (Phil. 2:13).
- We believe that humble, faithful planting and watering in reliance upon Jesus will yield fruit, even in the midst of painful controversy and resistance (Matt. 25:21; 1 Cor. 3:6).
- We believe that the cross of Jesus—the worst rejection, adversity, and opposition ever faced—and his triumph over death guarantee us that no labor in the Lord will ever be in vain (1 Cor. 15:58).

Spiritual leadership may be hard and heartbreaking, but it is always hopeful because of where the hope is anchored. Moses's reward was not in winning peoples' admiration, in wielding power, in the accumulation of earthly wealth, or even in the Promised Land. God was his reward. Moses considered that gaining God was such a reward that giving up all the wealth of Egypt and enduring the reproach of Christ throughout his vocational life was more than worth it all (Heb. 11:26).

Any servant-leader whose reward is God is equipped to weather the powerful and painful storms with overcoming faith and joy, even during sorrow (2 Cor. 6:10). A leader who pursues any other reward will not last.

"I have sinned, for I have transgressed the commandment of the LORD and your words, because I feared the people and obeyed their voice."

1 SAMUEL 15:24

6

YOU OBEY THE ONE YOU FEAR

KING SAUL AND FEAR OF MAN

Based on 1 Samuel 15

AT THE ROOT OF insecurity—the anxiety over how others think of us—is pride. This pride is an excessive desire for others to see us as impressive and admirable. Insecurity is the fear that instead they will see us as deficient. As King Saul shows us, insecure pride is a dangerous fear because insecurity can lead to great disobedience.

○○

Samuel's heart was broken and heavy as he neared Saul's camp at Gilgal. Israel's first king had failed so soon and so seriously.

And Samuel was tired. He'd been up all night, prayerfully mourning the Lord's words: "I regret that I have made Saul king, for he has turned back from following me and has not performed my commandments."[1]

And he was angry. The Lord had already severely disciplined Saul for officiating the burnt offering when he knew it transgressed the law (1 Sam. 13:8–14). But God had been gracious in giving him another chance by sending him to carry

---

[1] The quotations in this story are from 1 Samuel 15:11–24.

out judgment on the Amalekites. God made his instructions clear. Saul had not obeyed them.

The old prophet trembled at the word he must deliver to an armed king who feared public humiliation more than the Holy One.

Saul was all smiles when he saw Samuel approaching. "Blessed be you to the LORD. I have performed the commandment of the LORD," he shouted, as his entourage watched.

Samuel had to bite his tongue. "What then is this bleating of the sheep in my ears and the lowing of the oxen that I hear?" he said, with restrained but unmistakable displeasure.

Saul felt immediately exposed. Alone, he had figured that fudging some on the instructions really wouldn't matter. But now he knew he had gravely presumed. He fumbled for words. "They have brought them from the Amalekites, for the people spared the best of the sheep and of the oxen to sacrifice to the LORD your God, and the rest we have devoted to destruction."

This was a smoke screen, and Samuel knew it. "Stop!" Samuel cried. He could not bear Saul trying to cover disobedience with cosmetic righteousness. Or his cowardly hiding behind *the people*. "I will tell you what the LORD said to me this night."

Saul was defensive in his guilt. "Speak," he said loudly with a bravado disguise. The onlookers exchanged uncomfortable glances.

"Though you are little in your own eyes, are you not the head of the tribes of Israel?" Samuel asked sharply. "The LORD anointed you king over Israel. And the LORD sent you on a mission and said, 'Go, devote to destruction the sinners, the Amalekites, and fight against them until they are consumed.' Why then did you not obey the voice of the LORD?"

Looking over at the plump livestock, the price of Saul's kingdom, Samuel said, "Why did you pounce on the spoil and do what was evil in the sight of the LORD?"

Saul was defiant in his denial. "I *have* obeyed the voice of the LORD. I have gone on the mission on which the LORD sent me. I have brought Agag the king of Amalek, and I have devoted the Amalekites to destruction. But the people took of the spoil, sheep and oxen, the best of the things devoted to destruction, to sacrifice to the LORD your God in Gilgal."

Samuel let his head drop in frustration and disappointment. And he shook it with a subtleness that stung Saul as much as anything the prophet had said . . . yet.

Samuel's anger was mixing now with grief. With teary eyes still focused on the ground, he said, "Has the LORD as great delight in burnt offerings and sacrifices, as in obeying the voice of the LORD? Behold, to obey is better than sacrifice, and to listen than the fat of rams. For rebellion is as the sin of divination, and presumption is as iniquity and idolatry."

Samuel paused and caught his breath. Slowly he looked up into Saul's eyes, shy with guilt. "Because you have rejected the word of the LORD, he has also rejected you from being king."

Saul swallowed hard and nervously glanced at the wordless watching men around him. He was sweating. He leaned on his spear and looked at the ground. "I have sinned," he said quietly, "for I have transgressed the commandment of the LORD and your words, because I feared the people and obeyed their voice."

○ ○

Saul is a sober reminder to us that we obey the one we fear. Saul feared the people—he loved his reputation—and therefore despised God. Being little in our own eyes can be either righteous or ruinous. It's righteous if we see God as big and us as small. But it's ruinous if we see the approval of man as big and the commandments of God as small, because this always leads us to disobey God.

When we disobey, and all of us do at some point, God calls us not to mere remorse, but repentance. Saul was remorseful, but not repentant. He pursued his own glory in the praise of men over the glory of God in faithful obedience until his death on Mount Gilboa. He died a deeply insecure and lethally paranoid man.

Let us repent of our insecurities and say with Peter and the disciples, "We must obey God rather than men" (Acts 5:29). For the wise and humble "fear him who can destroy both soul and body in hell" (Matt. 10:28).

"Martha, Martha, you are anxious and troubled about many things, but one thing is necessary."

LUKE 10:41-42

7

WHOM ARE YOU REALLY SERVING?

MARTHA, MARY, AND SERVING

Luke 10:38–42

IN THE STORY OF Martha and Mary, Martha is not the strange one. Mary is.

The day Martha welcomed Jesus and his contingent into her home in Bethany, the group might have numbered a hundred or more. The seventy-two Jesus had sent out on itinerant ministry tours had just rejoined him. And considering his fame at this point, no doubt his visit to town attracted a number of locals.

After the group had packed inside, Jesus taught them. But Martha wasn't one of "them" because she was too busy to listen, "distracted with much serving" (Luke 10:40).

Now, removed from the situation, it's tempting to be condescending. *Oh, for goodness' sake, Martha! Jesus is in your house, and you're too busy to listen to him?*

But put yourself in Martha's place for a moment. How distracted would you be if a hundred people crowded into *your* home? Add to this the fact that as a first-century Near Eastern woman you would have a very high cultural value of hospitality and a keen fear of dishonoring guests, especially important ones. Then take that up a few notches as you remember that it's *Jesus* in your home. He's the Messiah, the most important person in your nation's history, and, in fact, human history.

Would you be distracted by how much you need to clean, or how much you need to cook, or how much food you need to buy, or how much water you need to bring from the well, or how many details you need to remember not to forget?

That's why I say that Martha isn't the strange person in this story. Mary is strange because she *wasn't* distracted. She ignored the insistent to-do lists so she could listen to Jesus.

And this irritated Martha. She was working like crazy while Mary just sat there. Martha considered this either laziness or negligence. Exasperated, she finally appealed to Jesus: "Lord, do you not care that my sister has left me to serve alone? Tell her then to help me" (Luke 10:40).

Now, Jesus loves to commend diligent servants:

> Who then is the faithful and wise servant, whom his master has set over his household, to give them their food at the proper time? Blessed is that servant whom his master will find so doing when he comes. (Matt. 24:45–46)

But in this case Jesus didn't commend Martha. He reproved her:

> Martha, Martha, you are anxious and troubled about many things, but one thing is necessary. Mary has chosen the good portion, which will not be taken away from her. (Luke 10:41–42)

To just about everyone else present, Martha's serving probably appeared to flow from the heart of a gracious servant. But Jesus discerned differently. He saw that Martha's serving flowed from anxiety, not grace.

What was making Martha anxious? We know she was anxious *about* "many things." But we need only examine our own similar anxieties to guess the likely root. I think Martha was anxious over how she impressed Jesus and her other guests. She was troubled at the thought that her home and serving might reflect poorly on her and her family. And this anxiety blinded her to the "one thing necessary"—listening to Jesus—and made many unnecessary tasks feel compulsively urgent.

This kind of anxiety is subtle. It has a selfish root but its fruit looks deceptively like unselfishness. This anxiety is the desire for approval dressed up to look like the desire to serve. This anxiety is my caring what you think of me dressed up to look like my caring for you. It can be so subtle that we don't see it clearly. It can look so much like the right thing that we believe it is the right thing. That's why Martha was confident that Jesus would agree with her about Mary.

But Mary had chosen the "one thing necessary," the "good portion." At that moment, Mary was more enthralled with Jesus than with Mary. She cared more about what Jesus said than what others thought of her, and because of this Jesus commended her choice not to serve.

Jesus's gentle rebuke of Martha was an act of love—to her and to us. We are all Marthas at times, and through her example Jesus is asking us, whom are we *really* serving in our serving? No one's motives are ever completely pure. But when we feel compelled to "serve" out of a self-conscious anxiety over what others think, we are serving our own glory and not Jesus's glory.

Jesus frees us from this slavery by inviting us to stop working, rest at his feet, and listen to him.

So he came to a town of Samaria called Sychar, near the field that Jacob had given to his son Joseph. Jacob's well was there; so Jesus, wearied as he was from his journey, was sitting beside the well. It was about the sixth hour. A woman from Samaria came to draw water.

JOHN 4:5–7

8

JESUS COMES WHEN YOU LEAST EXPECT

THE WOMAN AT THE WELL AND PERSEVERING PRAYER

Based on John 4:1–45

"**THE SON OF MAN** is coming at an hour you do not expect," Jesus said of his second coming (Luke 12:40). But Jesus showing up at unexpected times and places is a familiar pattern in his dealings with us in almost all areas of life. His reasons for this are mysterious and glorious, as the woman at the well in John 4 experienced.

Let's imagine this Samaritan woman many years later as Photine,[1] living in Rome and listening to a young friend, Clodia, expressing her discouragement in waiting on Jesus.

○○

Photine sensed Clodia's invisible burden. "What's on your mind, dear?"

"Nothing."

Photine looked around for the basket of pears and said, "Clodia, you know I won't accept that response." Spying the pears behind Clodia, she said, "And would you pass the pears, please?"

---

[1] Eastern Orthodox tradition says the woman at the well took the name *Photine* (or *Photini*), meaning "enlightened one," after her baptism, and that she became an effective evangelist, moved to Rome, and was martyred during Nero's persecution.

Clodia passed the basket. "OK, but I guess I'm telling the truth. *Nothing* is what I'm thinking about . . . as in nothing ever changes."

Photine laughed. "Oh, when you get to be my age, dear, you'll know that change is all that *ever* happens."

"Except the things you really *want* to change," muttered Clodia, dropping a handful of pistachios into a cloth bag.

Clodia was new to Rome, having recently moved from Carthage where she had become a Christian about six years earlier. The gracious, aged Photine had taken her under her wing. This morning they were preparing food for some of the sisters who had been jailed the previous week for sharing Jesus with a senator's daughter. Clodia didn't know all of Photine's past.

"I'm listening," Photine said, handing Clodia another bag.

"Jesus said if we ask the Father anything in his name he will give it to us," said Clodia (John 16:23). "And I've seen some answers to prayer. But I have so many things I desperately want him to change. I ask and ask and nothing seems to change. Some things have even gotten worse, not better." She filled the bag. "I don't understand it."

The old woman put three pears in the last bag and handed it to Clodia. "You will, honey, once you learn that Jesus is coming."

Clodia wasn't inspired. "I know Jesus is going to come back someday. But I'd like him to answer some of my prayers before then." In went the last fist of pistachios.

"I don't simply mean Jesus's return, dear," replied Photine. "I mean that Jesus is coming in answer to every righteous request you make in his name."

"What do you mean, he's coming?"

"He promised that your prayers would be answered, didn't he? Here, put those meal bags into this large sack. I'll put away the food." Photine groaned as she got up and stiffly carried the pear basket to the table. "You just need to learn to trust his timing."

"But if he's coming, why is he taking so long?"

"Sweetheart, he's God. Some prayers he answers in a day, some in a decade, some in a thousand years. Just set the sack by door." She came back for the bowl of pistachios. "Some prayers he answers after five marriages."

Clodia set the sack down and looked back at Photine, shocked. "What? Five marriages?"

"Five," answered the godly old woman, and she shook her head. "And after the fifth I stopped with the formalities." Clodia looked stunned. "Yes, I was the Whore of Sychar, Clodia, a slave to my sin. I prayed many times that God would deliver me, and saw nothing change. I heard that Messiah was going to come someday, but I stopped hoping that he'd ever come for me. And then, one day, when I least expected him, there he was, waiting for me beside a well."

Photine poured the nuts into the storage sack. "Many times since, he has come in answer to my prayers. But rarely when or how I expected him. Experience has taught me that his strange ways are always best, though. So don't stop praying, dear. But don't place your hope on time. Let Jesus mind the time, and you mind his faithfulness. He's never yet broken a promise. He will answer you."

○ ○

God is not deaf to your groaning prayers, the ones that come from the core of your being (Rom. 8:26). He knows your deep longings, your desires for his kingdom to come, your yearnings to be "set free from [creation's] bondage to corruption and obtain the freedom of the glory of the children of

God" (8:21). He is coming to fulfill every righteous desire beyond your wildest imaginings.

But "the Son of Man is coming at an hour you do not expect" (Luke 12:40). His timing is often mysterious to us, but he knows what he's doing. By employing the element of surprise in glorious purposes, he humbles human pride, catches Satan off guard (12:39), and, wonderfully, heightens our joy when the answers come.

So keep praying and cultivate patient, long-suffering faith. There will be a day when you find him unexpectedly at the well of your deepest thirst.

"So we labored at the work, and half of them held the spears from the break of dawn until the stars came out. I also said to the people at that time, 'Let every man and his servant pass the night within Jerusalem, that they may be a guard for us at night and may labor by day.' So neither I nor my brothers nor my servants nor the men of the guard who followed me, none of us took off our clothes; each kept his weapon at his right hand."

NEHEMIAH 4:21–23

9

WHAT GOD IS BUILDING THROUGH ALL THE INEFFICIENCIES OF LIFE

NEHEMIAH AND ADVERSITY

Based Mainly on Nehemiah 4

TIME IS MONEY. AND money is money. So when we want to get something done, we want it done as efficiently as possible.

That's why we are often bewildered when God gives us work to do and then allows the inefficiencies of trouble and opposition to consume so much time, energy, and money. Why does God let this happen? We see a clue in the book of Nehemiah.

When we first read of Nehemiah, God seemed to prosper everything he did. He rose through the ranks of Artaxerxes's court to the prestigious and highly trusted position of king's cupbearer. He enjoyed close proximity to, and high credibility with, the king. This in turn caused the king to notice Nehemiah's sadness over Jerusalem and want to do something about it.

Soon Nehemiah was off to Jerusalem with a royal leave of absence, a building permit, and a military escort. When he arrived, he quickly mobilized volunteers to rebuild sections of the city's crumbled wall. And these folks "had a mind to work" (Neh. 4:6). Things were going very well.

Then Sanballat and Tobiah entered the picture. Their peoples remembered Judah's former regional dominance. A rebuilt Jerusalem meant a national Jewish resurrection, and they were determined to keep that tomb closed.

They tried everything. They jeered, insulted, threatened attack, plotted assassinations, and intimidated Jewish families. They even threatened to tell Artaxerxes that his cupbearer had treasonous plans to appoint himself king of Judah.

But none of their plans succeeded. The "good hand of God" (Neh. 2:8) remained on Nehemiah and his crew.

Sanballat and his cronies, however, did slow the Jews' progress. Half of Nehemiah's reconstruction crew stopped building in order to stand guard, and the other half worked while carrying weapons. Even at night they remained battle-ready.

This was a costly distraction. Productivity would have probably tripled with focused, rested workers. God gave Nehemiah incredible favor with mighty Artaxerxes. Why did he not provide favor with Sanballat and Tobiah? Why did God allow so much wasted time, energy, and money?

The answer lies in the master Architect's design. In God's economy, none of these resources were wasted. He invested them in building something far more important and precious than a city wall. God was building faith.

A rebuilt city and a faithless people would not please God (Heb. 11:6). History had shown that a strong wall doesn't save "unless the Lord watches over the city" (Ps. 127:1). So as Nehemiah and the people worked to rebuild Jerusalem, God worked—through opposition—to build their dependent faith in his power rather than their own. It was the opposition that prompted Nehemiah to preach, "Do not be afraid of them. Remember the Lord, who is great and awesome" (Neh. 4:14).

Faith is "the conviction of things not seen" (Heb. 11:1). God gives faith as a gift (Eph. 2:8), but he tests, refines, and strengthens it in the fires of difficulty, adversity, opposition, and suffering. We learn to "walk by faith, not by sight" (2 Cor. 5:7) when we are forced to trust what is "not seen" more than what is seen.

That's why all the inefficient trials of our kingdom life and labor are not wasted. God is building "the tested genuineness of [our] faith," which he considers "more precious than gold" (1 Pet. 1:7). Trials, more than prosperity, teach us to "remember the LORD" (Neh. 4:14).

So "count it all joy" today "when you meet trials of various kinds" (James 1:2). God is building your faith.

Faith is worth all the time, energy, and money it costs to build.

"Oh, my Lord, please send someone else."

EXODUS 4:13

10

DON'T FEEL QUALIFIED FOR YOUR CALLING?

MOSES AND INADEQUACY

Various Texts

FOR THE FIRST FORTY years of his life, Moses lived in a place of strength. As a member of Pharaoh's household he had social prestige, wealth (Heb. 11:26), and youthful vigor. When he witnessed his people's oppression, Moses used this strength to exact vigilante justice on an cruel Egyptian (Ex. 2:12). But Moses's strength was not God's plan for deliverance, and Moses was forced to flee for his life.

So, having spent his first forty years in the palaces of Egyptian power, Moses spent his second forty years in the fields of Midian obscurity. Then one day he stumbled upon a burning bush, which turned out to be God's surprising call for his third forty years:

> Behold, the cry of the people of Israel has come to me, and I have also seen the oppression with which the Egyptians oppress them. Come, I will send you to Pharaoh that you may bring my people, the children of Israel, out of Egypt. (Ex. 3:9–10)

This call scared Moses out of his wits. So much so that he argued his case face-to-face with God. Let's listen in on the debate.

Objection 1: I'm a Nobody, God.

"Who am I that I should go to Pharaoh and bring the children of Israel out of Egypt?" (Ex. 3:11). Any fame or social credibility I may have once had is gone. In fact, I'm a shepherd and "every shepherd is an abomination to the Egyptians" (Gen. 46:34).

Objection Overruled: "I will be with you" (Ex. 3:12). Your calling is not based on your credibility, but on mine. I don't want Egypt or Israel impressed with you. I want them impressed with me.

Objection 2: They Aren't Going to Believe Me, God.

"But behold, they will not believe me or listen to my voice, for they will say, 'The LORD did not appear to you'" (Ex. 4:1). They're going to think I'm loony! I can believe in you myself, because you're revealing yourself to me. But we're up here on a mountain where no one sees. I'm still a nobody, and nobody's going to listen to a nobody's words, especially if he's claiming to speak for God!

Objection Overruled: "I will be with you" (Ex. 3:12). The same power that I demonstrate to you in secret I will demonstrate to them "that they may believe that the LORD, the God of their fathers, the God of Abraham, the God of Isaac, and the God of Jacob, has appeared to you" (Ex. 4:5). My point is to impress them with me, not you. Trust me, I will show up.

Objection 3: I Am Not Gifted to Do This, God.

"Oh, my Lord, I am not eloquent, either in the past or since you have spoken to your servant, but I am slow of speech and of tongue" (Ex. 4:10). I know the rhetorical expectations of Pharaoh's court. I mean, I wouldn't even qualify for *Midian's Got Talent*! Haven't you read the "know-your-strengths" books, God? I can't do this!

Objection Overruled: "Who has made man's mouth? Who makes him mute, or deaf, or seeing, or blind? Is it not I, the LORD? Now therefore go, and I will be with your mouth and teach you what you shall speak" (Ex. 4:11–12). You're still missing the point. I want Egypt and Israel to be impressed with me, not you. Don't be afraid. I will be with you and your unimpressive mouth.

Objection 4: Don't Make Me Do This, God.

"Oh, my Lord, please send someone else" (Ex. 4:13). Seriously, there's got to be a better candidate for this job! I might still be wanted in Egypt for capital murder. If not, I'm just a nobody. Worse, I'm a shepherd! And if it's not bad enough that I'm an obscure murdering abomination, I stumble all over myself when I speak publicly! I don't want this calling.

Objection Overruled: Enough! I have purposes in choosing *you* for this call. You don't know all those purposes yet, so stop leaning on your own understanding and trust me (Prov. 3:5–6). But since you have such little faith for this, I'll send your more eloquent brother, Aaron, with you, and "I will be with your mouth and with his mouth and will teach you both what to do" (Ex. 4:15). Now get moving!

○○

Do you feel unqualified for what God is calling you to do? Join the club. Kingdom work is supernatural work, no matter what your calling is. If it doesn't require real faith and a desperate dependence on God, then either it's not God's calling or you don't get it yet.

Have you been arguing with God over your calling qualifications? If so, remember Moses. And remember that God's call on you is not about you. It's about him. And the question is, are you willing for God to use your weaknesses to show how impressive he is?

God chose what is foolish in the world to shame the wise; . . . what is weak in the world to shame the strong; . . . what is low and despised in the world, even things that are not, to bring to nothing things that are, so that no human being might boast in the presence of God. (1 Cor. 1:27–29)

Don't use your weaknesses as an excuse for unbelief. Move forward in faith. God will be with you.

Demas, in love with this present world, has deserted me and gone to Thessalonica. . . . Get Mark and bring him with you, for he is very useful to me for ministry.

2 TIMOTHY 4:10-11

11

FAILURE DOESN'T HAVE TO BE THE LAST WORD

DEMAS, MARK, AND FAILURE

2 Timothy 4:10-11

DEMAS AND MARK ARE contrasts in failure. One provides us a word of warning, the other a word of hope. And as people who stumble in many ways (James 3:2), we need both.

Demas

What happened to Demas? We don't know, but we find a clue in a few heartbreaking words from Paul, some of the last he wrote before his Roman execution: "Demas, in love with this present world, has deserted me and gone to Thessalonica" (2 Tim. 4:10).

Maybe Demas feared being executed with Paul and fled to safety. Maybe he escaped to a place where he could let himself succumb to the siren song of immoral seduction. Or maybe he simply caved in to the allure of life in the urbane, cosmopolitan, pluralistic, wealthy, culturally interesting city of Thessalonica.

Whatever lured Demas away, Paul saw it as a love affair with the world.

Mark

But just a few sentences later in this letter to Timothy, Paul says something very hope-giving: "Get Mark and bring him with you, for he is very useful to me for ministry" (2 Tim. 4:11).

Remember Mark? He was the first to desert Paul. Back in the early days, on the very first missionary trip, Mark left Paul and Barnabas in Pamphylia and returned home to Jerusalem (Acts 13:13). Again, we don't know why. But Paul didn't approve. In fact, when Barnabas wanted to bring Mark back on the team after the Jerusalem Council, Paul said no way (15:37–40).

But now, at the end of Paul's life, Paul fully trusted Mark and called him "very useful" in the gospel ministry.

A Word of Warning

Demas is a warning to us. He began well. Four or five years earlier, during another imprisonment, Paul called Demas a "fellow worker" in the gospel (Col. 4:14; Philem. 1:24). There was a time when Demas apparently chose, like Moses, "rather to be mistreated with the people of God than to enjoy the fleeting pleasures of sin" (Heb. 11:25).

But Demas doesn't appear to have ended well. Having once fought kingdom battles alongside Paul, he deserted to the enemy's side.

Here's our warning: "Be sober-minded; be watchful. Our adversary the devil prowls around like a roaring lion, seeking someone to devour. Resist him, firm in your faith" (1 Pet. 5:8–9).

Our enemy is very real and very crafty. He threatens and seduces. And even leaders who start strong, like Demas, can fall to his deception. We must "fight the good fight of the faith" (1 Tim. 6:12) and do all we can do to stand firm (Eph. 6:13).

A Word of Hope

Mark, on the other hand, is an encouragement to us. He had a weak start. He didn't appear to have the right stuff. He disappointed his leaders and friends by leaving them to bear the heat of battle while he went home.

But Mark ended well. At some point he rejoined the battle and proved a faithful, trusted, useful warrior. And, if tradition is correct, the Lord even granted him the privileges of contributing to the New Testament canon, planting a church in Alexandria, and being martyred for the sake of Jesus.

Be Restored and Reenlist

All of us fail. And yes, some failures wreak horrible destruction. But if we turn from our sinful failures to Christ, there is no failure that can't be redeemed by the cross. And if we will wait for the Lord, there is no failure that Christ can't restore to useful service. Jesus chooses and uses failures. Paul knew this from personal experience:

> I thank him who has given me strength, Christ Jesus our Lord, because he judged me faithful, appointing me to his service, though formerly I was a blasphemer, persecutor, and insolent opponent. But I received mercy . . . (1 Tim. 1:12–13)

We don't know the last word on Demas. I hope that he repented in the end. But, as Mark shows us, we know that failure doesn't have to be the last word for us.

Whatever past or present failure confronts you, bring it to the cross and leave it. Desert it! Come, be restored by Jesus. If you've been AWOL in the fight of faith, come reenlist in the battle. It's not too late.

Forget what lies behind and strain forward to what lies ahead (Phil. 3:12). Resolve again to pursue Jesus as your treasure. And watch him redeem even your worst failures and make you very useful for ministry.

He said to them, "It is not for you to know times or seasons that the Father has fixed by his own authority."

ACTS 1:7

12

GOD IS MERCIFUL NOT TO TELL US EVERYTHING

THE DISCIPLES AND TRUST

Acts 1:6–8

WHEN GOD CHOOSES NOT to tell us everything, he shows us more mercy than we realize.

On the Mount of Olives with Jesus, just before his ascension to the Father, one of the disciples asked a question that must have been on everyone's mind: "Lord, will you at this time restore the kingdom to Israel?" (Acts 1:6).

It had been a long wait. Two thousand years had passed since God promised to give Abraham a seed that would bless all the families of the earth. Fifteen hundred years had passed since God told Moses that a great prophet would arise to lead the people, and a thousand years had passed since God promised to place an eternal heir of David upon the throne.

Now, after Jesus's triumphal resurrection, the disciples finally understood why the King had to suffer and die before the kingdom could really come. Jesus was the sacrificial Lamb of God whose death would atone for all the sins of all his people for all time.

It all made glorious sense.

So the stage looked set. Having conquered death, this King

was invincible. What threat was the Sanhedrin or Herod or Pilate or Caesar? Surely the time had come for the long-awaited King to assume his earthly reign, right?

Jesus's answer: "It is not for you to know times or seasons that the Father has fixed by his own authority. But you will receive power when the Holy Spirit has come upon you, and you will be my witnesses in Jerusalem and in all Judea and Samaria, and to the end of the earth" (Acts 1:7–8).

In other words, "Now is not the time. And you don't need to know when it will be. But for now, I have work for you to do."

Can you imagine how the disciples might have felt if at that point the Lord had explained to them that he would not assume his earthly reign for another two thousand-plus years, during which time the church would face delay and struggle and sacrifice as it spread around the world? Two thousand years?

God is merciful not to tell us everything. He tells us enough to sustain us if we trust him, but often that does not feel like enough. We really think we would like to know more.

In her book, *The Hiding Place*, Corrie ten Boom recalled a time when, as a young girl, she was returning home on the train with her father after accompanying him to purchase parts for his watch-making business. Having heard the term *sexsin* in a poem at school, she asked her father what it meant. After thinking for a bit, her father stood up and took down his suitcase from the rack. This is how Corrie remembers their conversation:

> "Will you carry it off the train, Corrie?" he said.
>
> I stood up and tugged at it. It was crammed with the watches and spare parts he had purchased that morning. "It's too heavy," I said.

"Yes," he said. "And it would be a pretty poor father who would ask his little girl to carry such a load. It's the same way, Corrie, with knowledge. Some knowledge is too heavy for children. When you are older and stronger you can bear it. For now you must trust me to carry it for you."[1]

God is also a wise Father who knows when knowledge is too heavy for us. He is not being deceptive when he does not give us the full explanation. He is carrying our burdens (1 Pet. 5:7). If we think our burdens are heavy, we should see the ones he's carrying. The burdens he gives to us to carry are light (Matt. 11:30).

God is very patient and merciful with us. Someday, when we are older and stronger, he will let us carry more of the weight of knowledge. But until then, let us trust him and thank him to carry our burdens.

---

[1]Corrie ten Boom, John L. Sherrill, and Elizabeth Sherrill, *The Hiding Place* (Grand Rapids, MI: Chosen, 1984), 42.

And Jesus said, "Who was it that touched me?" When all denied it, Peter said, "Master, the crowds surround you and are pressing in on you!" But Jesus said, "Someone touched me, for I perceive that power has gone out from me." And when the woman saw that she was not hidden, she came trembling, and falling down before him declared in the presence of all the people why she had touched him, and how she had been immediately healed. And he said to her, "Daughter, your faith has made you well; go in peace."

LUKE 8:45-48

13

JESUS IS TURNING YOUR SHAME INTO A SHOWCASE OF HIS GRACE

THE HEMORRHAGING WOMAN AND SHAME

Luke 8:42–48

YOU KNOW THAT PART of you that you *really do not* want others to see—that stubborn weakness, humiliating failure, embarrassing illness, horrible past event, or present struggle with sin? Luke 8 has very good news for you, in this healing story of a woman with a persistent sickness.

○○

Jesus was now a reluctant celebrity, and a crowd teemed around him as he made his way toward Jairus's home to heal the synagogue ruler's twelve-year-old daughter.

In the crowd was a desperate woman. For twelve years she had suffered from a vaginal hemorrhage. All the medical treatments she sought had bled her savings. Nothing had helped.

But she had seen Jesus's healing power. When he touched people, they were healed. If he could just touch her . . .

However, she had a problem. Her problem was the problem. Everyone who came to Jesus for healing had to tell him—

and thus everyone else—what his or her problem was. Jairus had just done that. But a vaginal discharge? In front of all those men? Even worse, her bleeding made her unclean, which added a deeper shame to her embarrassment.

But maybe Jesus didn't need to know that he touched her at all. What if she touched him? With that mass of people all trying to get close to him, she could just quickly touch his cloak. Nobody would ever know!

She pushed and jostled her way toward the Rabbi. The closer she got, the greater the knot in her stomach tightened. His disciples were trying to keep people from grabbing him, but her desperation fueled her determination. Suddenly there was an opening in the crowd and she quickly bent down and swept her hand along the edge of Jesus's cloak.

As she straightened up and stepped back, she felt a flash of heat through her abdomen. She knew instantly she was healed. A flash of shocked joy washed over her.

For about five seconds.

Jesus stopped and searched the crowd. He asked loudly, "Who was it that touched me?"

A flash of fear washed over the woman. Those closest pulled back from Jesus. Everyone looked at everyone else. There were various declarations of "I didn't do anything!" But the woman froze.

Peter, with some irritation, said to Jesus, "Master, the crowds surround you and are pressing in on you!" (Luke 8:45). For goodness' sake, everybody's trying to touch you!

But Jesus, still looking, said, "Someone touched me, for I perceive that power has gone out from me" (v. 46).

The woman realized she had been caught. It had never occurred to her that she might be stealing this healing.

Meekly she said, "It was me." She stepped back toward Jesus, and the crowd parted. In tears she dropped to her knees in front of him. "I touched you, Master." And she poured out her shame in front of everyone.

Jesus leaned toward her, wiped her tears, and said, "Daughter, your faith has made you well; go in peace" (v. 48).

oo

When Jesus finally got to Jairus's home and resurrected his daughter, he told her parents not to tell anyone (Luke 8:56). And yet this woman, who tried so hard to keep her healing a secret, was required to tell everyone. Why?

Because this woman *believed* in him.

In that moment, Jesus did not expose her weakness and shame. He exposed her faith. He wanted her faith visible so that everyone who carries a secret shame—which is every one of us—might have hope.

Jesus, the Great Physician, has the power to heal us from every sin, every weakness, every failure, every illness, and every evil ever committed against us. And he promises this healing to everyone who believes in him (John 3:16; Matt. 21:22).

Faith pleases God (Heb. 11:6), and faith releases the grace of God in your life (Eph. 2:8; Luke 8:48). Do you want deliverance from your shame? Come to Jesus *believing*. Come desperately determined to touch him. And if faith is weak, cry out, "I believe; help my unbelief!" (Mark 9:24) and "increase [my] faith!" (Luke 17:5).

No, not *every* promised grace will be received in this age (Heb. 11:39). In fact, most are being saved for your best life in the age to come (11:35).

But if you believe in him, you will receive sufficient grace (2 Cor. 12:9) to help you in your time of need (Heb. 4:16).

So trust him and take heart! Jesus will turn your place of shame into a showcase of his grace.

And Abraham said to God, "Oh that Ishmael might live before you!" God said, "No, but Sarah your wife shall bear you a son, and you shall call his name Isaac. I will establish my covenant with him as an everlasting covenant for his offspring after him."

GENESIS 17:18-19

14

GOD'S MERCY IN MAKING US FACE THE IMPOSSIBLE

ABRAHAM, SARAH, AND FAITH

Shortly after Genesis 17:22

GOD IS NOT CONTENT for us just to understand the *idea* that nothing is too hard for the Lord (Jer. 32:17). He wants us to have the overwhelming joy of *experiencing* it. But the some-times-agonizing period between his promise and his provision can push us to the brink of what we *think* we can believe, as it did for Abraham and Sarah.

○ ○

Abram entered the tent, his eyes on the ground, his mind a world away. He was breathing hard. Sarai was repairing a cloak. She watched him as he walked to the back corner and collapsed on the cushions with a sigh. She recognized the bodily weari-ness of a divine encounter.

"The Lord has spoken to you again, hasn't he?"

There was a pause.

"Yes."

It usually took Abram a while before he could talk about these encounters, so Sarai pulled her threadwork up close again where she could see—another reminder of her aging body. But now her hands were trembling. She dropped them back into her lap. What had the Lord said?

"Ishmael!" Hagar was calling her son, and the name pierced through Sarai like an arrow. She looked through the open flap and saw Hagar hand her son supplies to carry to the cooking fire. The boy was thirteen and beginning to look like a man. He was his father's delight, the flesh of his flesh. But not of hers. The Lord had promised Abram offspring. But it was a deep, bewildering grief that he had granted it through Hagar, her own maidservant. And worse, it had been her own idea.

"Sarah."

She looked over at Abram. What had he just called her?

"Yes, I called you Sarah. The Lord has changed your name."

The Lord spoke of her? Her heart sped with a rush of hope-fueled adrenaline.

"He changed my name? What do you mean?"

"You are not merely a princess. You will be the mother of kings."

Sarah stared. His words didn't register. A childless mother of kings?

"The Lord said, 'I will bless her, and moreover, I will give you a son by her. I will bless her, and she shall become nations; kings of peoples shall come from her' [Gen. 17:16]. Sarah, God is going to give you a son, and through him, nations."

Sarah's whole being staggered. She steadied herself with her left hand and cupped her mouth with her right. Tears streamed. Grief, hope, and confusion churned inside her. A child? She had tried to bury this desire, and she felt fear at resurrecting it. Besides, she was *ninety*. She hadn't had a feminine cycle for years. How could this possibly . . .

"I know what you're thinking. I thought the same thing. When the Lord spoke it, it was too much to take in, and I said to him, 'Oh that Ishmael might live before you!'"

The familiar pain shot through Sarah again.

"But God said, 'No, but Sarah your wife shall bear you a son, and you shall call his name Isaac.'"

Isaac. Her desire now had a name. Sarah mouthed it, but still had no voice.

"Yes. Because the whole idea seemed so ludicrous that I laughed to myself."

"But . . . I can't . . . Husband . . . I'm ninety years old." Sarah began sobbing. "My body is no longer able to bear children. My time has passed."

Abram walked over and enveloped his wife in his arms. "I know, Sarah. We are powerless to have children, now more than ever. But if we've learned anything these twenty-five years, it's that our hope doesn't rest on our power to do anything. Our hope rests on the Lord's power. Our entire lives are built on what he's promised. And the lives of our descendants must be built on his promises for generations before they ever occupy this land. Their survival will depend on them trusting the Lord's promises and not their own power. Should it really surprise us that the first descendant the Lord gives us is a reminder of this?"

Sarah leaned into her husband.

"And, my precious wife, our Isaac will always remind us, and many after us, that the Lord makes us laugh at the impossible."

"Your faith strengthens mine, Abram."

"Abraham."

Sarah looked up at him, puzzled again.

"Yes, the Lord changed my name, too." Abraham smiled. "A mother of nations needs a father of nations, doesn't she?"

○ ○

Sometimes our difficult circumstances make it seem impossible for God to fulfill his promises. When we find God's promises unbelievable, as did Abraham (Gen. 17:17–18) and Sarah (Gen. 18:11–14), God has exposed the boundaries of our faith—boundaries he means to expand.

Learning to rest in the promises of God occurs in the crucible of wrestling with unbelief—seasons, sometimes long seasons, when everything hangs on believing that God "gives life to the dead and calls into existence the things that do not exist" (Rom. 4:17).

If you're in such a season, as difficult as it feels, God is being incredibly kind to you. Because it is in such seasons when we *really* learn that nothing is too hard for the Lord (Gen. 18:14).

Abraham and Sarah "grew strong in [their] faith" (Rom. 4:20) because God pushed them to believe more than they thought was possible. For the sake of our joy, he does the same for you and me.

By faith Abraham, when he was tested, offered up Isaac, and he who had received the promises was in the act of offering up his only son, of whom it was said, "Through Isaac shall your offspring be named." He considered that God was able even to raise him from the dead, from which, figuratively speaking, he did receive him back.

HEBREWS 11:17–19

15

GOD WILL NEVER, NEVER BREAK HIS PROMISE

ABRAHAM, ISAAC, AND GOD'S FAITHFULNESS

Based on Genesis 22

HOW MIGHT ISAAC HAVE explained to his young sons, Jacob and Esau, why God had commanded his father, Abraham, to offer him as a burnt offering?

○ ○

Eight-year-old Esau sat on his bed-mat firing imaginary arrows in the dark at his younger twin, Jacob, who could hear him making his *pheoo* sound with each shot. They were hitting the target.

"Esau, stop!"

Pheoo.

"I said, stop!"

Pheoo.

"Stoooooop!"

Jacob's protests were aimed at his father's ears. They too were hitting the target. Soon the familiar scraping footsteps approached the tent. Esau lay down quickly, pretending to sleep. Father Isaac swept the flap aside and said firmly, "Sons of mine, that's enough. You're disturbing the whole camp. It's late. Go to sleep."

"Father, tell Esau to stop shooting at me!" complained Jacob.

"You have a shield, Jacob. It's called *ignoring him*. Use it."

"He's just doing it to make me mad!"

"Yes, and you're rewarding his effort," Isaac said. "Esau." Only silence. "Don't pretend you're sleeping, Son. Answer me."

"Yes, Father," Esau answered.

"Now stop," Isaac couldn't help letting a chuckle slip, "stop shooting your brother."

There was a giggle in the darkness. "Yes, Father," said Esau.

"Father?" Jacob asked.

"Yes, my son."

"Was Grandfather Abraham really going to stab you with the knife?" The boy had been pondering the strange, disturbing story his father had told them the previous night.

Isaac walked in and knelt between the boys. "He would have if God had wanted him to."

"Did God really want him to?" asked Jacob.

"That's a good question," replied Isaac. "What God really wanted was for Father Abraham to trust him, even if it meant sacrificing me."

"Did you know Grandfather Abraham was going to sacrifice you?"

"No. I noticed we didn't have a lamb. But when I asked him about it he said, 'God will provide for himself the lamb'" (Gen. 22:8).

It was quiet for a moment, and then Jacob asked, "Did that mean you were the lamb?"

"Well, it looked like I was going to be the lamb. But the main thing is that Father Abraham trusted that God would provide the lamb, and he was willing for me to be the lamb if that's what God required."

"But if you had died, Esau and I wouldn't have been born."

Isaac paused thoughtfully. "I don't think that's true, Jacob. Because God had made a promise to Father Abraham. Do you remember? God said, 'Through Isaac shall your offspring be named' (Gen. 21:12). When God makes a promise, he never breaks it. That means he knew I would grow up and have offspring and that you two scoundrels would be my offspring."

"But if you died, you couldn't have offspring!" Jacob objected.

"I know it sounds strange, Son. Here's how Father Abraham explained it to me: he believed so strongly that God would keep his promise that even if God was asking him to sacrifice me, then God must have planned to bring me back to life from the dead."

Esau interjected, "Like a ghost?"

"No, not like a ghost. God would have healed me and made me alive again, just like I am now."

Jacob continued, "But he didn't do that. God made a ram get caught in the bushes."

"That's right," said Isaac. "God provided a sacrifice just like he promised. And it wasn't me, God be praised!"

"But why did God tell Grandfather Abraham to make you the sacrifice if he already knew he was going to provide the ram?" asked Jacob perceptively.

"Well, I don't know all of God's reasons, Son. He always has more reasons than he tells us. But remember what I told you last night. After Father Abraham offered me, God said to him: 'By myself I have sworn, declares the LORD, because you have done this and have not withheld your son, your only son, I will surely bless you, and I will surely multiply your offspring as the stars of heaven and as the sand that is on the seashore. And your offspring shall possess the gate of his enemies, and in your offspring shall all the nations of the earth be blessed, because you have obeyed my voice' [Gen. 22:16–18]. So, Jacob, you tell me: Why did God tell Father Abraham to offer me as the sacrifice?"

Jacob thought for a moment. "To see if Grandfather would obey him?"

"Yes. Very good. But it was also to show us—me and you and Esau and your children someday—what it means to trust God. Father Abraham trusted God so much that he was willing to even sacrifice the fulfillment of God's promise—me—because he believed that God would still fulfill his promise. I want you to understand this, because the promise God made to Father Abraham he's also making to you: 'in your offspring shall all the nations of the earth be blessed.' Someday you're going to have to trust that God will keep his promise even when it looks like he won't. When that happens, remember Father Abraham and say with him, 'The LORD will provide' [Gen. 22:14]. Does that make sense?"

"Yes, Father," said Jacob.

"Now, what the Lord wants to provide for you tonight is sleep. So let's have it quiet."

Two tired voices responded, "Yes, Father."

As soon as Isaac's footsteps faded away Jacob heard an irritating sound in the dark.

Pheoo.

○ ○

As Abraham walked toward Mount Moriah with Isaac, he must have felt deeply conflicted and heartbroken beyond words. He didn't understand all that God was doing. He didn't know he was providing an illustration of justification by faith for God's people for all time (James 2:21–23). He didn't know this act would foreshadow the sacrifice of God's only Son—a Son who would *not* be spared because he *was* the provided Lamb (John 1:29).

Abraham only knew that God knew what he was doing, and that God could be trusted to keep his promise, even if it appeared like the promise was going to die (Heb. 11:19). And God proved himself faithful to Abraham.

God will prove himself faithful to you as well. Even if it doesn't look like it right now, God has his reasons, and they are more than you know. Trust him.

"Blessed are you, Simon Bar-Jonah! For flesh and blood has not revealed this to you, but my Father who is in heaven."

MATTHEW 16:17

"Get behind me, Satan! You are a hindrance to me. For you are not setting your mind on the things of God, but on the things of man."

MATTHEW 16:23

16

WATCH YOUR MOUTH

PETER AND BEING SLOW TO SPEAK

Based on Matthew 16:13–27

AS CHRISTIANS, WE ARE still vulnerable to Satan's deception. Our weakness is humbling. One moment we can speak words of glorious biblical truth, and the next moment we can spew words of destructive, satanic lies. We must set a guard over our mouths (Ps. 141:3). Peter learned this lesson the hard way.

○ ○

The disciples wondered why Jesus led them up to Caesarea Philippi. At the foot of Mount Hermon in the far north of Palestine, the population was mostly pagan. The people believed a legend that the Greek god, Pan, was born in a nearby cave that housed a great spring of water, so they built temples and shrines into the cliffs. Philip the Tetrarch made the city his capital, which he named in honor of Tiberius Caesar—and himself.

But for Jesus, Caesarea Philippi was likely a refuge from the needs of the pressing crowds and the controversy of the inquiring Jews. In this peaceful retreat he asked his disciples a defining question.

"Who do people say that the Son of Man is?" (Matt. 16:13).

"John the Baptist," answered one. Others stifled laughs,

because John had died only a few months ago. But the strange rumor had made Philip's half brother, Antipas, tremble (Matt. 14:2).

Another said, "Some say Elijah." This answer made more sense, since the prophet, Malachi, had said Elijah would come (Mal. 4:5). But in John the Baptist "Elijah" had died a few months ago.

"Or one of the other prophets, like Jeremiah," said a third.

Jesus seemed to be lost in thought for a few minutes. Then he looked around the group and asked, "But who do you say that I am?" (Matt. 16:15).

This question pierced right to their deepest hope. It was a hope their ancestors had nurtured for centuries—a hope that had been dashed many times. It was a hope so dear that, even after all of Jesus's signs, most were hesitant to say it.

But not Peter. For right or wrong, he was bolder than the rest. "You are the Christ, the Son of the living God," he answered, with characteristic conviction (Matt. 16:16). The words echoed off the rocky walls. Every man felt his diaphragm tighten. This was the moment of truth. Their hopes rested on Jesus's response.

Jesus looked at Peter, as affection spread across his face. "Blessed are you, Simon Bar-Jonah! For flesh and blood has not revealed this to you, but my Father who is in heaven" (Matt. 16:17).

Awe permeated this holy moment. Before Peter's declaration, Jesus had all but proclaimed himself the Messiah. But now the line had been officially crossed. Peter said what they all desperately hoped was true. And Jesus affirmed it.

With those blessed words, Peter earned his name. From then on he was a memorial stone of the mammoth, Mount Hermon–like truth of Jesus's person and his mission—the indestructible truth on which the church would be built.

But then irony struck. The rock of truth quickly became a stumbling block.

After declaring himself the Messiah, Jesus immediately began explaining to his disciples that his mission required his capture, death, and resurrection. They did not hear Jesus's plans as good news. How in the world could the messianic kingdom be established if the Messiah died?

Peter was disturbed. It wasn't like Jesus to sound so resigned to being overcome by evil. There was no way that God would allow his Son to be killed and leave all the prophecies unfulfilled. Hadn't they experienced God's omnipotent power? And if it was a matter of protection, well, Jesus needed to know that no one would lay a hand on him except over Peter's dead body!

At the next opportunity, Peter took Jesus aside and said, "Far be it from you, Lord! This shall never happen to you" (Matt. 16:22)

Jesus cut him off with intense authority: "Get behind me, Satan!" There was no affection this time. "You are a hindrance to me. For you are not setting your mind on the things of God, but on the things of man" (Matt. 16:23).

Peter stepped back, confused. This was the last thing he expected to hear from Jesus. Satan? He was being used by Satan? He thought he was just trying to help.

○ ○

Peter learned a life-shaping lesson in that moment. He might have recalled Jesus's words later in life, when he wrote this exhortation:

> Be sober-minded; be watchful. Your adversary the devil prowls around like a roaring lion, seeking someone to devour. Resist him . . . (1 Pet. 5:8–9)

As Christians, the Holy Spirit reveals to us, and even communicates through us, some of the most glorious truths of Scripture. Yet we still must watch our mouths, not only to refrain from harsh words of impatient irritability or selfish ambition, but also, as in Peter's case, to avoid spreading sincerely held misunderstandings. Satan is subtle. He is very good at deceiving us where our understanding is limited or partial. If we are not careful, we can be fully convinced that we are advancing God's kingdom when we are really opposing it.

This is why it is important that we be "quick to hear, slow to speak" (James 1:19). There is a good reason the Bible tells us to "incline [our] ear to . . . understanding" (Prov. 5:1). We are frequently wrong in our initial perceptions, and we bring all sorts of presuppositions and biases to "[our] own understanding" (Prov. 3:5). If we are quick to speak, and slow to listen, we will find ourselves, however unintentionally, a satanic stumbling block for others.

Jesus wants us to listen carefully and ask lots of questions so that we really understand before we speak confident assertions. This is part of what it means to be clothed with humility, because, as Peter both experienced and later wrote, "God opposes the proud but gives grace to the humble" (1 Pet. 5:5).

And they discussed it among themselves, saying, "If we say, 'From heaven,' he will say to us, 'Why then did you not believe him?' But if we say, 'From man,' we are afraid of the crowd, for they all hold that John was a prophet." So they answered Jesus, "We do not know."

MATTHEW 21:25-27

17

HOW JESUS EXPOSES OUR IDOL OF SELF-GLORY

THE JEWISH LEADERS AND REPUTATION

Matthew 21:23–27

THE LOVE OF OUR own glory is the closest competitor with God in our hearts. And sometimes we cloak our self-worship in a pious disguise. In Matthew 21, Jesus exposed this idol in the hearts of a few men with just a single question.

○○

It was the final week before Jesus's day of judgment—the day he would stand before his Father's bar of justice, bear the sins of all who ever had or would believe in him, and endure the Father's wrath in their place.

Jesus no longer avoided the treacherous Jewish political and religious leaders. He openly confronted their errors and duplicity, pouring fuel on their fiery hatred and fear of him.

In the eyes of the Jewish leaders, Jesus was out of control. He had been a growing problem for a couple of years, but on Sunday he wreaked havoc in the temple, driving out the sacrifice merchants as if he owned the place—shortly after riding into Jerusalem like a king, to the wild cheers of thousands. Many of the crowd proclaimed him the Messiah, and he did not refute them!

The leaders rejected Jesus as the Christ. After all, he was

from godforsaken Galilee (John 7:52). And this blasphemer and chronic Sabbath-breaker called *them* hypocrites!

Now Jesus was a full-blown crisis. If they didn't take decisive action soon, the Romans would get involved.

The problem was the crowd. They had to find a way to win the people to their side.

After some deliberation, the Jewish leaders conceived a question that would surely hang Jesus on the horns of a dilemma. Either answer would incriminate him, divide the crowd, and give them cause to arrest him.

On Monday morning, as Jesus was teaching in the temple, the appointed delegation made their way to him through the crowd. The spokesman asked loudly, "By what authority are you doing these things, and who gave you this authority?"[1]

Jesus leaned back and squinted up at them. The tension was thick.

Shielding his eyes from the morning sun, he answered, "I also will ask you one question, and if you tell me the answer, then I also will tell you by what authority I do these things. The baptism of John, where did it come from? From heaven or from man?"

This was a stunning counter. Their concerned glances at each other said it all: he had caught them completely unprepared. The crowd began to murmur. Their hesitation was humiliating.

They huddled for a quick conference. "If we say, 'From heaven,' he will say to us, 'Why then did you not believe him?' But if we say, 'From man,' we are afraid of the crowd, for they all hold that John was a prophet." How had Jesus managed to flip the dilemma horns around on them?

They decided not to grab either horn. "We do not know." It was a politically expedient and, in their view, unavoidable lie.

---

[1] The quotations in this story are from Matthew 21:23–27.

Restrained anger flashed in Jesus's shielded eyes. "Neither will I tell you by what authority I do these things."

○ ○

Had the Jewish leaders been sincere, their question would not have been a wrong one. These men were supposed to guard God's truth and God's people. That's why Jesus was willing to answer. But his prerequisite question revealed that their apparent truth-guarding was a sham.

John the Baptist's love for God's glory and truth cost him his head. Jesus's love for God's glory and truth would cost him death on a Roman cross. Jesus's question was designed to reveal whether these leaders loved God's glory and truth more than public approval. If they answered him straight, he would give them a straight answer.

But they were "afraid of the crowd." In other words, they loved human approval and their own reputations more than they loved the truth—more than they loved God. So they "exchanged the truth about God for a lie" (Rom. 1:25).

We must remember that we do the same thing every time we distort or deny the truth for the sake of people's approval. Our idol of self-glory is revealed whenever the Lord presents us with an opportunity to glorify him by speaking the truth about our convictions or our sins, yet we fail to speak for fear of what someone else will think of us.

We have all sinned in feeble attempts to glorify ourselves. So thank God for the cross that covers such sins! "If we confess our sins, he is faithful and just to forgive us our sins and to cleanse us from all unrighteousness" (1 John 1:9).

Let us resolve not to fear people more than God and to be rigorously truthful in what we profess or confess. Let us love God's glory more than our own.

And as he was setting out on his journey, a man ran up and knelt before him and asked him, "Good Teacher, what must I do to inherit eternal life?"

MARK 10:17

18

THE IMPOVERISHING POWER OF FINANCIAL PROSPERITY

THE RICH YOUNG MAN AND WEALTH

Mark 10:17–31

THE STORY OF THE rich young man in Mark 10 has a clear, sobering message: earthly prosperity can make people spiritually destitute.

∞

"Teacher! Teacher, please wait!"

Jesus and his disciples were just leaving town. They turned and saw a young man hurrying toward them. His clothes, carriage, and elocution all communicated "aristocrat." But his face was distressed, and there was urgency in his voice. The disciples assumed someone else needed healing or deliverance.

The man dropped to his knees in front of Jesus and blurted out, "Good teacher, what must I do to inherit eternal life?"[1] Unusual. Not many wealthy people were so earnest about such things. The disciples looked back at Jesus. Still trying to figure out this question themselves, they were eager for his answer.

---

[1] This and the following quotations in this chapter are from Mark 10:17–27.

Jesus looked intensely at the young man for a moment. Then he said, "Why do you call me good? No one is good except God alone." Not the expected reply. The disciples were getting used to this, but the man just looked confused.

Jesus let his comment sink in for a bit. Then he said, "You know the commandments: Do not murder, Do not commit adultery, Do not steal, Do not bear false witness, Do not defraud, Honor your father and mother." At the time, the disciples didn't notice, but later, they discussed the commandments that Jesus didn't mention, like "you shall have no other gods before me" (Ex. 20:3). Another lesson learned: even what Jesus *doesn't* say means something.

The man replied, "Teacher." (He was careful to leave off "good" this time.) "All these I have kept from my youth." Remarkable. Most people desperate to talk to Jesus were either sick, demonized, or sinners looking for forgiveness. Why was a pious young man so troubled about his soul?

Jesus paused again, and his face radiated affection. The disciples anticipated a word of commendation or comfort. But what came out of Jesus's mouth was, "You lack one thing: go, sell all that you have and give to the poor, and you will have treasure in heaven; and come, follow me."

All eyes moved back to the young man. They watched blood and hope drain out of his face. His head drooped and he stared at the ground.

The man was devastated. He had known something was wrong, but he hadn't been able to put his finger on it. Most folks who knew him thought he was a good boy and told him that his wealth was God's blessing. But he hadn't been able to shake this nagging sense of guilt, even with all the rituals. He had hoped Jesus would give him the answer. But he wasn't prepared for *this* answer. However, now he knew why his soul was troubled. All it took was a clear choice between two treasures: God or wealth. There, on his knees in the dirt before Jesus, he realized which treasure he loved more. And it wasn't God.

He slowly got up, and without making eye contact, walked away still burdened.

Jesus watched him. Quiet murmuring began. Then he said, "How difficult it will be for those who have wealth to enter the kingdom of God." The hush was tense. With pain in his eyes, Jesus said, "Children, how difficult it is to enter the kingdom of God! It is easier for a camel to go through the eye of a needle than for a rich person to enter the kingdom of God."

The disciples gave each other unsettled glances. Each of them was suddenly very aware of idolatrous cravings in his heart. One of them said, almost under his breath, "Then who can be saved?" The question did not escape Jesus's ear. With unexpected joy he said, "With man it is impossible, but not with God. For all things are possible with God." And he set off down the road.

○○

According to Jesus, earthly prosperity is extraordinarily dangerous. It makes it humanly impossible to enter God's kingdom. It is fool's gold. But its power is so blinding that when Jesus held out real treasure to this man in exchange for the counterfeit, he wouldn't trade. And he chose poverty over incalculable eternal wealth.

Idols are not to be toyed with. They are to be destroyed. If financial security is an idol for us, Jesus will call us, in some way, to abandon it.

If you are in a place where God is asking you to trust and treasure him over money, remember that it is a great mercy. You might feel like you're in a "fiery trial" (1 Pet. 4:12) because you're being asked to die to what you once believed would bring you life. Don't be surprised "as though something strange were happening to you." Jesus is showing you the path of life (Ps. 16:11). He is offering you a priceless gift. Trust him. God can make a camel pass through a needle's eye, for all things are possible with him.

And Jonathan, Saul's son, rose and went to David at Horesh, and strengthened his hand in God. And he said to him, "Do not fear, for the hand of Saul my father shall not find you. You shall be king over Israel, and I shall be next to you. Saul my father also knows this." And the two of them made a covenant before the Lord. David remained at Horesh, and Jonathan went home.

1 SAMUEL 23:16–18

19

THE POWERFUL GLORY OF YIELDING POWER

JONATHAN AND POWER

Based on 1 Samuel 23:15–18

PERHAPS THE ONLY THING harder for us prideful humans than humbly *wielding* power is humbly *yielding* power. The most beautiful Old Testament example of giving up power is the way Jonathan yielded Israel's throne to David. As we see in 1 Samuel 23, Jonathan did far more than just *yield*.

Abinadab watched his fugitive younger brother receive Jonathan like royalty.[1] Such an embrace. Such intimate talk. Such weeping in farewell. What had David divulged to the enemy's son?

He stepped beside David at the cave's entrance and watched Jonathan depart. Abinadab pondered Jonathan's return to serve beside his father whose homicidal paranoia was forcing them to run like foxes and live like badgers.

"David, you won't like my asking, but I need to. Is it wise to just let him go back to Saul?"

---

[1] Abinadab was David's older brother, the second of Jesse's eight sons (see 1 Sam. 16:8).

"My life is never safer than when it's in Jonathan's keeping."

Abinadab shifted uneasily. "I know you love him. You're very loyal, and it's one of your great qualities. I just hope your loyalty isn't naive here."

David said nothing, his eyes still fixed on Jonathan.

Abinadab continued, "Brother, these are treacherous days. You barely escaped Doeg's loose tongue [1 Sam. 22:9–19]. And those cowards of Keilah would have offered you as a peace offering to Saul, despite the fact that you had just saved their necks from the Philistines [1 Sam. 23:1–4]. We need clear thinking here. Jonathan is next in line to be king. I know you've been friends. But the fact is, you're now his one rival to the throne. Isn't it possible that the blood of royal power may be thicker for Jonathan than the water of your friendship?"

Jonathan's silhouette melded into the dusky shadows of the Horesh hills. David wiped his eyes and turned back into the cave. "You don't know him, Abinadab. I'll forgive this offense to his honor. We're no more in danger than if that were our father walking away. But it's not Jonathan's affection for me that I trust. It's his faith."

Abinadab followed David. "Well, I hope I'm wrong, I really do. But Jonathan's coming out here makes no sense to me if it's not to spy you out. If he wanted to protect you, he should never have come at all! What if he was followed?"

"Nobody's more skillful at traceless trekking than Jonathan."

"Maybe. But why would he come just for a friendly visit? Think of the risk. If his father finds out that he was here and didn't report it, his life won't be worth a pigeon's. The king has nearly murdered him twice already![2] If he came here for love, then he risked his life and all of ours. Why?"

"To strengthen my hand in God, Abinadab. Because Jon-

---

[2] See 1 Samuel 14:24–46; 20:30–34.

athan knows me. He knows how discouraged I get." David looked down and smiled. "God sent him because *he* knows how dark it's been for me. I know what God has promised me. But with barely a step between me and death, it's like I just forget."

David sat down on a rock near his gear and pulled some parchment from his satchel. "I've been working on this psalm. Let me read you the first lines:

> My God, my God, why have you forsaken me?
> > Why are you so far from saving me, from the words of
> > > my groaning?
> O my God, I cry by day, but you do not answer,
> > and by night, but I find no rest. (Ps. 22:1–2)

"Today," David paused, clenching back sobs. "Today, Jonathan risked his life to help me rest—to remind me that God is not far at all. What he said to me was, '*Do not fear, for the hand of Saul my father shall not find you. You shall be king over Israel.*'" David paused again as tears flowed freely. "'*And I shall be next to you. Saul my father also knows this*'" (1 Sam. 23:17).

"Jonathan believes God, Abinadab. It's his faith I trust. Jonathan loves God more than he loves power. And more than he loves me. He loves me because he loves God. That makes him the safest man in the world to me. He has no equal." David hung his head. "I only hope he survives his father's insane faithlessness. I so desperately want him next to me."

○ ○

David had a very difficult calling: to *wield* the power of Israel's kingship with God-dependent humility.

Jonathan's calling may have been more difficult, however: to *yield* the power of Israel's kingship with God-dependent humility.

Jonathan didn't just yield to David. He loved David (1 Sam. 18:1), empowered David (v. 4), and protected and advocated for David (chap. 20). And when David's faith-hand was losing its grip, Jonathan sought him out and "strengthened his hand" by reminding him of God's promises (23:16–17). He could have done this only if he trusted in the Lord with all his heart (Prov. 3:5).

Like Jonathan, God wants us to seek first the kingdom, not our prominence in the kingdom (Matt. 6:33). When we trust God enough to yield our prominence (or expected prominence) to someone else for God's purposes, it's a sign and wonder. And when we go beyond yielding to doing everything in our power to help that person succeed—nothing else quite portrays the Philippians 2 glory of Jesus:

> Have this mind among yourselves, which is yours in Christ Jesus, who, though he was in the form of God, did not count equality with God a thing to be grasped, but emptied himself, by taking the form of a servant, being born in the likeness of men. And being found in human form, he humbled himself by becoming obedient to the point of death, even death on a cross. (Phil. 2:5–8)

Jonathan did not consider the throne a thing to be grasped, but he emptied himself for God's sake and became a Christlike servant. Let us also "have this mind" (Phil. 2:5).

"Do not call me Naomi; call me Mara, for the Almighty has dealt very bitterly with me."

RUTH 1:20

20

WHEN IT SEEMS LIKE GOD DID YOU WRONG

NAOMI AND TRAGEDY

Ruth 1

THE STORY OF NAOMI in Ruth 1 teaches us that how things *look* and how things *feel* are often not how they *are*.

○ ○

The last time Naomi saw her hometown on the Judean hillside, the barley fields were barren in the House of Bread.[1]

The famine had stirred the specter of starvation. Naomi's husband, Elimelech—not a patient man even in bounty—was convinced that Moab held a better life. Moving to Moab had frightened Naomi nearly as much as starvation. The Moabites did not fear Yahweh. They worshiped the bloodthirsty god, Chemosh. Naomi prayed desperately for a full harvest to keep them home, but Yahweh had not moved. So her man of action had moved her, their two sons, and the necessities they could carry to Moab.

Now, a decade later, Naomi was returning home. The Bethlehem barley fields were full and ripe. But her house was now

---

[1] The Hebrew name *Beyth Lechem*, which we pronounce *Bethlehem*, means "house of bread."

barren. In Moab, she had suffered a famine of men. So as her friends greeted her, she replied, "Do not call me Naomi [*pleasant*]; call me Mara [*bitter*], for the Almighty has dealt very bitterly with me" (Ruth 1:20).

It *had* been a hard ten years. Elimelech died only a year after they had settled. But with a crop in the ground and famine still ravaging Judah, Naomi was trapped.

More Moabite chains fastened on her when her sons Mahlon and Chilion each married Moabite women. She had grieved this deeply at first. But Ruth and Orpah had surprised her. They proved to be solaces, not sorrows. Quickly she had come to love them like daughters.

Especially Ruth. How such a woman had come to Mahlon was a marvel. Naomi had never known anyone like her. Ruth was unusually kind and wise beyond her years. And she proved to be the hardest worker in the household. Ruth was an oasis of joy in Naomi's Moab wilderness.

But the Lord brought disaster on Naomi again when Mahlon and Chilion died just weeks apart. Their deaths left her destitute. Loveless, manless, wealthless, she was left with nothing in a land that cared nothing for her.

What added to the cruelty was that her sons' deaths would strip her of Ruth and Orpah, the only two left in that godforsaken place who *did* care. It felt like driving two more knives into her heart, but with no way to support them, she knew she had to send them away. Their best chance for salvaged lives was to return to their fathers' homes and hope to marry again someday. Her best chance was to go home and hopefully live off the goodwill of anyone in Elimelech's clan who had any.

The girls took her decision hard. They wept together over their dead and over the death of the life they had known. Both young widows feared for Naomi's survival and expressed their willingness to stay with her. But Naomi would not hear of it. And Orpah knew she was right.

But not Ruth. Ruth would not hear of leaving Naomi. When Naomi pressed her, Ruth made a vow—to *Yahweh*: "Your people shall be my people, and your God my God. Where you die I will die, and there will I be buried. May the LORD do so to me and more also if anything but death parts me from you" (Ruth 1:16–17). Such a vow could not be broken, and Naomi both rejoiced and grieved over it.

And she marveled again. Why would this young Moabitess, who excelled all other women, cast her lot with a hopeless old widow and a God whose favor seemed clearly to have been withdrawn?

The odd thing was that in Ruth's favor on her, Naomi recognized the faint scent of Yahweh's favor. But she fought against hope. What harvest could possibly spring up from the seeds of all those tragic tears sown over the past ten years?

○ ○

When Naomi arrived in Bethlehem after her sorrowful sojourn in Moab, she could not see a harvest from her tears. It all looked like a tragedy, like "vanity and a striving after wind" (Eccl. 1:14).

That's how it *looked*. That's how it *felt*. But that's not how it *was*.

In reality, all of the ups and downs in Naomi's life—the famine, the move to Moab, the deaths of Elimelech, Mahlon, and Chilion, Ruth's loyalty, Naomi's return at barley harvest, Boaz, and the kinsman who chose not to redeem Ruth—all of these events played parts in God's plan to redeem millions and weave a Moabite into the royal, messianic bloodline. The bigger story of redemption was far bigger than they imagined. Even though they were in the middle of the story, none of them could see it from their vantage point.

We must remember this perspective in our times of desolation, grief, and loss. How things appear to us, and how they actually are, are rarely the same. Sometimes it looks and feels like the Almighty is dealing "very bitterly" with us, when all the while he is doing us and many others more good than we can imagine.

God's purposes in the lives of his children are *always* gracious. Always. If they don't look like it, don't trust your perceptions. Trust God's promises. He is *always* fulfilling his promises.

And Simeon blessed them and said to Mary his mother, "Behold, this child is appointed for the fall and rising of many in Israel, and for a sign that is opposed (and a sword will pierce through your own soul also), so that thoughts from many hearts may be revealed."

LUKE 2:34–35

21

WHEN A SWORD PIERCES YOUR SOUL

MARY AND GRIEF

Based on Luke 2:22–35

GRIEF FEELS LIKE A sword piercing our soul, but God can use grief to unleash grace in our lives. As Mary learned, the event that caused her most the soul-piercing grief unleashed more grace, salvation, and joy into the world than she could have ever imagined.

It was midmorning when Joseph and Mary and their infant son entered Jerusalem's Fountain Gate at the city's southern tip. They passed the pool of Siloam where disabled and diseased ones hoped for a healing stir of the water, and walked northwest up the street that led to the Temple Mount. The city bustled with the rattle and hum of morning chores and commerce.

Forty days had passed since Mary birthed her boy. Under the law, the birth had made her unclean and required a purification sacrifice on the fortieth day. She and Joseph made the ten-mile trek from Bethlehem the previous day, camping with a few others a half mile or so outside the holy city.

Just outside the temple complex, Joseph bartered with

merchants for two turtledoves. The inflated prices angered him. Profiting from purification! He felt shame that he couldn't afford a lamb; doves were a poor man's sacrifice. He was barely eking out a living in Bethlehem, taking whatever odd job he could find.

Mary watched Joseph return with the cloth bag, its erratic movements divulging an inner turmoil. Sorrow flashed through her. She always recoiled at the sacrifices: the struggle, the fear, the violence, the blood. Innocent life killed because of another's guilt. These two frightened creatures would soon die to make her clean. She held Jesus tighter.

They entered the complex and made their way across the noisy Court of the Gentiles toward the Eastern Gate of the inner wall. Hundreds were praying, men with covered and women with uncovered heads.

Suddenly in front of them an old man appeared. "Let me see the child!" He sounded almost distressed. Joseph stepped up and shielded his wife. The man looked up at Joseph, confused, and then he smiled. Taking Joseph's prohibiting hand in both of his, he patted it and said, "I'm sorry, my son. You must forgive old Simeon. Please don't be afraid. Your child is in no danger from me. I've just been waiting for him so long."

Mary knew immediately that he knew. The old man looked to her and gently asked, "May I see your son?" Mary smiled and nodded. Joseph stepped back. The man moved near and looked in awe at the child. Barely audible he muttered, "The salvation of Israel. The glory of Israel."

Without taking his eyes off Jesus, he asked, "May I hold him?" Mary felt no fear as she placed Jesus into Simeon's arms. He gently rocked him, mouthing silent praise and streaming joyful tears. Mary glanced at Joseph who was wordless too.

Then the old man broke into a half-sobbing prayer, "Lord, now you are letting your servant depart in peace, according to your word; for my eyes have seen your salvation that you have prepared in the presence of all peoples, a light for revelation to the Gentiles, and for glory to your people Israel" (Luke 2:29–32).

Mary again felt the shivering wonder that her baby, this one she nursed and changed and bathed and cradled, was "Christ the Lord" (Luke 2:11).

Still gazing adoringly at the child, Simeon said, "Years ago the Lord promised me that death would not come until I had seen his Christ. Today I opened my eyes while praying and there you were—an infant! I had never thought you would be an infant!" Looking to Joseph with laughing eyes, he said, "One never thinks of the Christ as an infant!"

With a kiss of blessing, Simeon softly placed Jesus back in his mother's arms. He dried his eyes with the edge of his sleeve and turned to Joseph with a look of reluctant intensity. He laid a hand on Joseph's shoulder and said, "Behold, this child is appointed for the fall and rising of many in Israel, and for a sign that is opposed . . . , so that thoughts from many hearts may be revealed" (Luke 2:34–35).

Turning back to Mary, Simeon gently cupped her face with his kind hands and said tearfully, "And a sword will pierce through your own soul also" (Luke 2:35). He kissed her forehead, and with one last look at the child, he moved away slowly through the crowd.

○ ○

"A sword will pierce through your own soul." The most wonderful, gracious event in human history was God sending his Son into the world—to the cross—to "save his people from their sins" (Matt. 1:21). Yet this same gracious event caused indescribable grief for Mary.

As God works out his salvation of sinners, he leads us along unexpected paths that sometimes result in agonizing grief. When pierced with pain, we can remember Mary. The darkest moment of her life, the sword that stabbed deepest into her soul, was the moment that God used most to bring salvation and joy to the world—and to *her*!

That's how God works with us, too. When the sword pierces, all we feel is terrible pain. But later we discover that our deepest wounds can become the channels through which profound grace flows.

Then [Samson's] brothers and all his family came down and took him and brought him up and buried him between Zorah and Eshtaol in the tomb of Manoah his father. He had judged Israel twenty years.

JUDGES 16:31

22

THE WEAKNESS OF THE WORLD'S STRONGEST MAN

SAMSON AND UNFAITHFUL FAITH

Based on Judges 13–16

WHEN THE WRITER OF Hebrews listed the Old Testament heroes of faith, he included Samson (Heb. 11:32). We can be tempted to ask, "Really?" Samson's story, recorded in Judges 13–16, reads like the story of a narcissistic superhero whose pride destroys him in the end.

But God wanted Samson included in the list because his example teaches us crucial lessons about faith. To explore these, let's imagine two of Samson's brothers (I've given them the fictitious names Abijah and Nadir) on their way to collect Samson's body in Gaza (Judg. 16:31). As they reflect on all that went wrong in Samson's life, we can reflect on all that God did right in the greater storyline of faith.

○ ○

The two brothers said nothing for a long time after the ruins of Dagon's temple came into view. It lay on the ground like a torn carcass, and those still living were crawling through the debris extracting the dead.

They had come to retrieve their oldest brother, Samson, who's broken body still lay somewhere in the rubble. No Philistine had dared touch the cursed corpse of the man who with the strength of a god had brought the temple crashing down, taking more than a thousand of his mockers with him into the dark land.

When the brothers neared the ruins, they stopped to rest, and to muster some courage. Removing the body would be risking violent retribution from grieving Philistines.

Nadir, the younger of the two, broke the silence. "Did you ever think it would end like this?"

Abijah, seven years older, gulped down some water and handed the skin to Nadir. He answered, "I used to think he was invincible. I can still see him describing how he killed the lion barehanded. I was fifteen and almost worshiped him. He was so strong, so fearless. And God was with him. This," he said, nodding toward the wreckage, "would have been inconceivable to me back then, Samson dying blind in the house of Dagon."

"Why did God let this happen?"

"I'm sure the Almighty has reasons that I'll never know," Abijah replied. "But I think we need to be careful where we lay the blame. It wasn't God who was unfaithful."

"But I don't get it," Nadir said. "How can an angel foretell his birth, and how can God use him so powerfully, just to have his legacy collapse like this in the end?"

Abijah squinted toward the ruins. "It's probably too early to call this the end. God will use Samson's story more than we think. But our brother's life collapsed under the weight of his pride. God gave him an amazing gift, but he let that gift go to his head. I think he saw it as God's personal endorsement of him. He assumed God would keep blessing him, even though one by one he broke every Nazirite vow [Judg. 13:7]." Looking back at Nadir, he said, "God may be slow to anger [Ex. 34:6], but it's a dangerous thing to mistake God's *patience* with sin as a *license* to sin."

"But why did God keep blessing him when Samson was faithless?" asked Nadir.

"I wouldn't say that he was faithless," Abijah responded. "You can exercise faith while being unfaithful. Samson knew his strength came from God. He believed the angel's prophecy, and he believed that God would bless his gift of strength when Samson needed it. In that sense, every mighty act our brother ever did was by faith. And God used him."

"So by unfaithful, you mean what?" asked Nadir.

"I mean that Samson believed God would be faithful to his word, but Samson didn't believe he needed to be faithful to God's word. He trusted God to empower his gifting, but he didn't trust God to satisfy his appetites. So he disobeyed God and indulged sin. He was already blind when the Philistines finally got to him."

"I still don't understand why God kept blessing him when he was sinning," persisted Nadir.

Abijah answered, "If by *blessing* you mean Samson's strength, it was because God was being faithful to his word. He promised he would use Samson to deliver Israel from the Philistines (Judg. 13:5), and he faithfully kept that promise, even when Samson disobeyed him. And God was amazingly patient with him. He gave him so many chances, but Samson ignored them. When he finally broke the last vow, God's patience was over.

"The tragedy of our brother's life is that he ended up thinking more highly of himself than of God." Abijah looked back toward temple remains. "To me, that shattered temple is a monument to what happens when we are unfaithful with God's gifts."

○ ○

Samson is an unnerving hero of faith. He did exercise faith. But he was unfaithful in the most important thing: the love for God that's revealed in obedience (John 14:15). If we have great faith, but not love, we are nothing (1 Cor. 13:2).

God gives each of us gifts "according to the grace given to us" (Rom. 12:6). They are *grace* gifts (undeserved), and they are for the "common good" (1 Cor. 12:7). They are about God's greatness, not ours. They should keep us humble (Rom. 12:3), especially when we remember that some will stand before Jesus having done "mighty works" and God will say, "I never knew you" (Matt. 7:23).

So let Samson's faith soberly remind us that our talents or spiritual gifts are not God's endorsement of us. Faithful obedience is better than impressive giftedness, and that faith must work through love (Gal. 5:6).

Then the Lord said to Cain, "Where is Abel your brother?" He said, "I do not know; am I my brother's keeper?" And the Lord said, "What have you done? The voice of your brother's blood is crying to me from the ground."

GENESIS 4:9–10

By faith Abel offered to God a more acceptable sacrifice than Cain, through which he was commended as righteous, God commending him by accepting his gifts. And through his faith, though he died, he still speaks.

HEBREWS 11:4

23

WHAT DEAD ABEL SPEAKS TO US

ABEL, CAIN, AND FAITH

Based on Genesis 4 and Hebrews 11:4

THE STORY OF CAIN and Abel in Genesis 4 tells much more about Cain than Abel. In fact, not one word is recorded from living Abel. But the author of Hebrews says that "through [Abel's] faith, though he died, he still speaks" (Heb. 11:4). So what is Abel telling us?

○○

It was dusk. Cain was working late. Not wanting to face his parents, he was trying to disguise his guilt-infused fear with a preoccupation with his crops. Suddenly, the unmistakable voice of the Lord sent a shock through Cain's core: "Where is Abel your brother?" (Gen. 4:9).

Cain had grown to loathe Abel. No matter what, Abel always seemed to turn a situation to his advantage. Was there a conflict? Abel "the humble" loved to be the first to reconcile. Did anyone need help? Abel "the servant" loved to be the first to offer it. Was there an injury? Abel "the compassionate" loved to be the first to comfort. Even when Cain showed greater endurance and ingenuity in his work, Abel "the virtuous" could rob him of any satisfaction with virtuoso performance of self-effacement.

Most maddening for Cain, however, was Abel "the pious," flaunting his tender conscience and precious devotion to God for the admiration of all. Cain could barely stomach how his father and mother gushed over that.

With every perceived humiliation, Cain fertilized the secret suspicion that Abel only used goodness to show himself superior to Cain.

But that morning Cain suffered a crushing blow. The Lord required each brother to present an offering, the first fruits of their labors, and Cain saw in this an opportunity. This time Abel would not upstage him. Cain would prove that he, too, could excel in devotion. So he made sure that his offering lavishly exceeded the required amount of his best produce.

But when the Lord reviewed Cain's extravagant offering, he rejected it. Cain was stunned. Then, adding injury to insult, the Lord accepted Abel's comparatively simple lamb offering. Humiliated by Abel again! But this time before God!

Cain's hatred metastasized into horror. Abel had outshined him for the last time. By late afternoon Abel's lifeless body lay in a remote field, abandoned in the hope that a beast's hunger would conceal the fratricide.

But the Lord's question left Cain "naked and exposed" (Heb. 4:13). He lied with the anger of cornered guilt: "I do not know; am I my brother's keeper?" (Gen. 4:9). What Cain did not know, in fact, was that his silenced brother had not been quiet. The Lord replied, "What have you done? The voice of your brother's blood is crying to me from the ground" (v. 10).

○○

The blood of dead Abel cried out to God for justice (Gen. 4:10; Heb. 12:24). But the faith of dead Abel "still speaks" (Heb. 11:4). So what is Abel saying to us through his faith?

Without Faith It Is Impossible to Please God

One thing we hear is that *God only accepts faith-fueled offerings.* It's significant that God doesn't provide details about either Cain's or Abel's offerings, the first ever recorded in the Bible. In the story, I imagine Cain trying to win God's approval with an impressive looking offering. But it could just have easily been a stingy offering or an exactingly precise offering. The point is that, right from the beginning, God draws our attention away from what fallen humans think is important (how our works make us look impressive) to what God thinks is important (how our works reveal who we trust).

All of Scripture teaches that "the righteous shall live by his faith" (Hab. 2:4) because "without faith it is impossible to please" God (Heb. 11:6). Abel was "commended as righteous" by God because he presented his offering in faith (Heb. 11:4). Cain's offering was "evil" (1 John 3:12) because without humble trust in God, even our offerings (hear: any work we do for God) are evil to God—even if they appear to everyone else as obedient or impressive.

You Will Be Hated by All for My Name's Sake

A second thing we hear from Abel is that *the world will hate you if you live by faith in Jesus* (whom the New Testament reveals is Yahweh, the Lord [Phil. 2:11]. The apostle John makes this hatred clear: "We should not be like Cain, who was of the evil one and murdered his brother. And why did he murder him? Because his own deeds were evil and his brother's righteous. Do not be surprised, brothers, that the world hates you" (1 John 3:12–13). Abel was the first to discover that "all who desire to live a godly life in Christ Jesus will be persecuted" (2 Tim. 3:12).

To "let [our] light shine before others, so that they may see [our] good works" (Matt. 5:16) will at times expose others' wickedness and arouse their hatred (John 3:20). Jesus himself said, "You will be hated by all for my name's sake," and "some of you they will put to death"—some even at the hands of "parents and brothers and relatives and friends" (Luke 21:16–17). Righteous faith arouses evil hatred.

A Better Word Than Abel's Blood

In the story, though we'd rather see ourselves as Abel, we are all Cain. We were all at one time cursed, "hostile to God" and alienated from him (Rom. 8:7; Eph. 4:18). Abel, the first martyr of faith, is a foreshadowing of our Lord Jesus, whose "blood . . . speaks a better word than the blood of Abel" (Heb. 12:24). For though Abel's innocent blood cried out for justice against sin, Jesus's innocent blood cried out for mercy for sinners. Abel's blood exposed Cain in his wretchedness. Jesus's blood covers our wretchedness and cleanses us from all sin (Rom. 7:24; 1 John 1:9).

So now, as we seek to present our bodies as living sacrifices to God, let us remember that the only thing that makes our offerings acceptable to God, the only thing that makes our sacrifices a spiritual service of worship, is our childlike faith in Jesus (Rom. 3:26; 12:1). And let us soberly remember that the only reward we are likely to earn from the world is its hatred.

And God said to Noah, "I have determined to make an end of all flesh, for the earth is filled with violence through them. Behold, I will destroy them with the earth. Make yourself an ark of gopher wood."

GENESIS 6:13-14

24

THE FOLLY OF WHAT NOAH PREACHED

NOAH AND GOSPEL BOLDNESS

Sometime during Genesis 6

PAUL WROTE, "FOR THE word of the cross is folly to those who are perishing, but to us who are being saved it is the power of God" (1 Cor. 1:18). In Noah, we have an Old Testament illustration of this truth. Ponder how Noah's warnings about fantastic "events as yet unseen" (Heb. 11:7) must have sounded to his hearers. I've imagined the responses of two of Noah's neighbors, fictitiously named Talmai and Bakbukiah.

○ ○

"This is madness!" Talmai was alarmed by the huge piles of logs strewn around the vast clearing and all the hired men cutting and hauling them. "How long will this boat be?"

Noah braced for a deluge of ridicule. "Three hundred cubits."

"Unbelievable!" laughed Bakbukiah. "Three hundred? You were right!" he said slapping Talmai's back. "I said, 'No one's *that* stupid.' But I stand corrected."

Talmai shook his head in disbelief. "Noah, you've lost your mind! No one can build a boat that big."

"You are an idiot!" shouted Bakbukiah. "You're building a three-hundred cubit boat six-day's journey from the sea?"

"It won't need to be near the sea," Noah replied.

"Oh, come on, Noah," sighed Talmai. "You've been preaching about this flood of divine judgment. But look around! You seriously believe all this is going to be under water?"

"Talmai, I don't base my faith merely on what seems plausible to me," said Noah.

"Well, that's obvious!" scoffed Bakbukiah.

Noah held up his hand and continued, "I base my faith on what God says he will do."

"Whose god, Noah?" asked Talmai flatly.

"The only God there is, Talmai: Elohim, the Almighty, the Creator," said Noah.

"So Elohim is a mass murderer then?" said Bakbukiah mockingly.

"Bakbukiah, you're speaking foolishness," said Noah.

"*I'm* speaking foolishness?" snapped Bakbukiah. "You're building a colossal boat in the middle of nowhere because some bloodthirsty god told you to, and you're calling *me* foolish?"

"Yes, I am! Because you're assuming that what *looks* foolish to you *is* foolish," replied Noah.

"Building this ark doesn't just *look* foolish, Noah," said Talmai curtly.

"Tell me what foolishness is, Talmai," countered Noah.

"Foolishness is *that*, my friend," said Bakbukiah, gesturing toward the site.

"No, I want you to answer the question. What *is* foolishness?" said Noah.

"It's believing something that isn't real!" exclaimed Talmai. "Basing your life on a delusion!"

"Exactly!" said Noah. "Foolishness is basing your life on a delusion."

Both men looked at Noah for a moment, perplexed.

Talmai snorted. "You're saying that we're the deluded ones?"

"Yes. What makes you certain that you're not deluded?" asked Noah.

"Common sense, Noah. Try it! Comes in handy in boat building," chortled Bakbukiah.

"Common sense? Whose common sense, Bakbukiah?" responded Noah. "Yours? The common sense you exercise when beating your wives when you're angry? Or when you try to take advantage of your customers? Or perhaps it's the common sense of your friend, Jobab, who extorted sex from the wife of a man indebted to him? Or the common sense of that man who cut Jobab's throat? Or, Talmai, was it your common sense in working your slave into the ground and beating him mercilessly for petty infractions? Or was it your slave's common sense in raping your daughter before he escaped? Or, Bakbukiah, was it the chief's common sense to run your father through with a spear for mocking him?"

"Watch your tongue, old man, if you want to keep it," threatened Bakbukiah.

"Point made then," replied Noah. "Depravity is rampant everywhere. Look at us. We always carry our weapons because we can't trust anyone. And when we're honest, we know *we* aren't trustworthy. The most common sense we share is our evil selfishness."

"Listen, that's beside the point," asserted Talmai. "The point is there isn't going to be any flood and this huge ark is a waste of time, money, and trees."

"It's not beside the point," said Noah. "Elohim has been warning us for generations to forsake our evil, self-absorbed sin and return to him. No one has listened! We have only gotten worse. We're consuming each other! The point is that your perception of reality is distorted by self-centeredness, Talmai.

Elohim created the predictable world that you know. And it's foolish to presume that he can't unexpectedly turn this plain into a sea."

"Well, if he does, this Elohim of yours is as wicked as the rest of us. He's just going to drown us all like dogs," replied Bakbukiah. "Except you, of course, because you're so righteous."

"Not true, Bakbukiah. It is not Elohim's bloodthirst and selfishness that is bringing the flood. It's his justice. It's what our sin deserves. Don't you see? In his mercy he has been warning us over and over. But the ark is a sign that he will not wait forever. And God isn't sparing me because my nature is any better than yours. He's sparing me because I *trust* him. I believe what he says. And this ark will shelter *anyone* who will trust him. Join me, brothers! You don't have to perish in Elohim's judgment. Believe him and escape!

Talmai looked blankly at Noah. "Build your boat, crazy man. But keep away from me and my family."

"Me too," added Bakbukiah. "If Elohim's going to wipe out everyone I know and love, then I want to go where they're going. I'm not going on a boat ride with a murderous god, religious fanatics, and a bunch of wild animals!"

○○

The clever and contemptuous mockery of those who find the gospel simply ridiculous stings us. Their derision can stir up fears and doubts that we might really be foolish after all, and their scorn can tempt us to keep our mouths closed.

God knows all our fears, doubts, and temptations, and reminds us that the gospel will sound foolish to the world because he's "[making] foolish the wisdom of the world" (1 Cor. 1:20). Then he repeatedly tells us not to be ashamed of it (Luke 9:6; Rom. 1:16; 2 Tim. 1:8).

Like Noah, who was a "herald of righteousness" in his age (2 Pet. 2:5), we also are heralds of "events as yet unseen" (Heb. 11:7). Jesus tells us that Noah's flood was a foreshadow:

> For as were the days of Noah, so will be the coming of the Son of Man. For as in those days before the flood they were eating and drinking, marrying and giving in marriage, until the day when Noah entered the ark, and they were unaware until the flood came and swept them all away, so will be the coming of the Son of Man. (Matt. 24:37–39)

But in this greater judgment a greater, more perfect Ark has been provided: the crucified and risen Son of Man. All who are in him when the flood of God's wrath comes will be saved. But only those who believe his Word can enter this Ark.

If Noah's warning and gospel sounded foolish to his hearers, how much more does our warning and gospel sound to our hearers? We must not be surprised when others ridicule it, for "the word of the cross is folly to those who are perishing" (1 Cor. 1:18). But "it pleased God through the folly of what we preach to save those who believe" (v. 21).

Our call is not to be respected by the unbelieving world. Our call is to trust the Lord's Word over the confident contempt of those who are blinded (2 Cor. 4:4). Our call is to endure the reproach Jesus endured (Heb. 13:13), and preach the gospel for the sake of "[those] who are being saved" (1 Cor. 1:18).

That same night the LORD said to him, "Arise, go down against the camp, for I have given it into your hand. But if you are afraid to go down, go down to the camp with Purah your servant. And you shall hear what they say, and afterward your hands shall be strengthened to go down against the camp." Then he went down with Purah his servant to the outposts of the armed men who were in the camp. And the Midianites and the Amalekites and all the people of the East lay along the valley like locusts in abundance, and their camels were without number, as the sand that is on the seashore in abundance.

JUDGES 7:9-12

25

WHY GOD GIVES US MORE THAN WE CAN HANDLE

GIDEON AND THE IMPOSSIBLE

Based on Judges 7

THE NEXT TIME SOMEONE says that God doesn't give us more than we can handle, point them to Judges 7. God instructs Gideon to take on over one hundred thousand enemy soldiers with just three hundred of his own, placing this story directly in the "more than you can handle" category. Imagine how Gideon and his servant, Purah, must have felt, trying to come to grips with their humanly impossible assignment.

○ ○

Standing on the side of Mount Gilboa, Gideon gazed over the Plain of Jezreel, which sprawled beneath him northward toward the Hill of Moreh. The plain was a sea of tents, teeming with Midian warriors.

That morning, the Lord judged Israel's army of thirty-two thousand too big to face Midian's one hundred thousand warriors. Even outnumbered three to one, Israel would "think of himself more highly than he ought to think" when God gave him victory (Rom. 12:3). So Gideon had announced that whoever was afraid was free to go home. When twenty-two thousand soldiers took him up on the offer, Gideon had to quiet his own fear. Now Israel was outnumbered more than ten to one. But God was with them, and he had overcome such odds before.

Oddly, the Lord considered these odds still too much in Israel's favor. So in obedience to the Lord's instruction, Gideon brought his small, thirsty army down to the spring of Harod. And he gave his servant, Purah, the strangest command of his brief military career: "Observe all the men as they drink. Have every man who laps his water like a dog stand off to the side."

Gideon supervised the selection, but when he saw so few being chosen, he just let Purah finish the count, and he climbed back up Gilboa to pray and survey.

It wasn't long before Purah emerged from the trees.

"So what's the total?"

"Three hundred, sir," said Purah.

Gideon chuckled to himself. "Three hundred." He looked back toward the human horde in the valley and was quiet for a moment. "That's less than I expected."

"Yes, sir," said Purah. "Thankfully, three hundred doesn't reduce our strength much."

Gideon breathed deeply. "No, Purah. The three hundred are not the reductions. They are the army. The others are the reductions."

Purah stood dazed for a moment, staring at Gideon. "The three hundred are the army?"

Gideon nodded slowly, still looking into the Midian-infested plain.

"But that's not an army! That's how many should be guarding the army's baggage!"

Purah stepped up beside Gideon. Together they watched smoke columns rising from ten times more cooking fires than they now had warriors. Purah shook his head and said, "Even if we were all like the mighty men of old, three hundred cannot overcome one hundred thousand." He paused. "And we are not mighty men." Another pause. "And there are more than one hundred thousand down there."

Both were silent for a while. In the quiet, the Lord spoke to Gideon, "With the three hundred men who lapped, I will save you and give the Midianites into your hand, and let all the others go every man to his home" (Judg. 7:7).

Then Gideon said to Purah, "During the exodus, how many mighty men did it take to destroy the Egyptian army or part the Red Sea?"

Purah thought briefly. "None."

"How many did it take to tear down Jericho's walls?"

"None."

"How many did it take to feed two million people in the wilderness every day for forty years?"

"None. I get your point."

"In our people's history, the mightiest have not been the strongest," Gideon said. "The mightiest have been those who trusted in the Lord and obeyed him, no matter how impossible things appeared. God has promised us that Midian will be defeated. He has chosen only three hundred of us. We will obey; he will act. And when Midian falls, it will be clear to everyone *who* felled him." Then he looked at Purah and smiled. "Maybe the Lord just needs us to guard his baggage!"

Purah didn't laugh. He only replied, "We should dismiss the others then?" Gideon nodded.

Later that night, in the tiny camp, Gideon lay praying. Every plan to mobilize three hundred against one hundred thousand seemed ludicrous.

Suddenly, he was aware of the Presence. He sat up, his heart racing.

The Lord said, "Arise, go down against the camp, for I have

given it into your hand. But if you are afraid to go down, go down to the camp with Purah your servant. And you shall hear what they say, and afterward your hands shall be strengthened to go down against the camp" (Judg. 7:9–11).

Gideon nudged Purah and whispered, "Let's go."

"Where are we going?" Purah whispered back, getting up quickly.

"To the Midian camp, just you and me. The Lord has something he wants to show us."

They quietly crept toward the nearest Midian outpost, veiled by the clouded sky, and saw two inattentive guards talking. Just as they got within earshot one said, "I had a strange dream before being woken for duty tonight."

"Tell me," the other said.

"This cake of barley came tumbling into our camp, crashed into the tent, turned it over, and flattened it."

The other guard looked at him, alarmed, and said, "I know what that means! The cake can be none other than Gideon, the son of Joash! God has given us all into his hand!"

Gideon and Purah looked at one another with the same stunned expression.

○○

With renewed faith, Gideon and Purah roused their mini-army and launched a night attack. Their surprise threw the Midians into a panic, and they slaughtered each other in confusion. It was a rout. Not one of Gideon's three hundred perished in the battle.

God gave Gideon's army more than they could handle to force them to rely wholly on him.

When we're confronted with an impossible situation or trial, Gideon's three hundred soldiers preach to us that "salvation . . . is from the LORD" (Ps. 37:39) and that "if God is for us, who can be against us?" (Rom. 8:31). God does not intend for these verses to be mere platitudes. He intends for us to cast all our anxieties on these massive truths, and to receive more-than-conquerors' confidence and peace, no matter what we face (v. 37).

It is not hyperbole to say that Jesus's defeat of our sin dwarfs Gideon's defeat of Midian. Compared to overcoming God's wrath against our sin, defeating one hundred thousand Midianites is very small. And if God "did not spare his own Son but gave him up for us all, how will he not also with him graciously give us all things?" (Rom. 8:32).

God certainly does give us more than we can handle. And he does it "to make us rely not on ourselves but on God who raises the dead" (2 Cor. 1:9). If you're facing overwhelming adversity and you wonder how God can possibly deliver you and work it for your good (Rom. 8:28), then take heart from Judges 7, Romans 8, and 2 Corinthians 1. When God gives you more than you can handle, he is giving you the joy of experiencing his power to do the humanly impossible "so that your faith might not rest in the wisdom of men but in the power of God" (1 Cor. 2:5).

Barak said to [Deborah], "If you will go with me, I will go, but if you will not go with me, I will not go." And she said, "I will surely go with you. Nevertheless, the road on which you are going will not lead to your glory, for the Lord will sell Sisera into the hand of a woman."

JUDGES 4:8-9

26

IMITATE, DON'T IDOLIZE, YOUR LEADERS

BARAK AND MISPLACED FAITH

Based on Judges 4–5

BARAK WAS A HERO of early Israel, serving during the premonarchy period when Deborah judged the nation. His great military feat was the complete rout of the Canaanite general, Sisera, and his army. In the process, Barak learned the important distinction between *imitating* and *idolizing* the faith of a leader he respected.

Deborah sat praying on the roof of Barak's house in the small lakeside village of Kedesh-naphtali. The afternoon shadows from the southwest hills lengthened into evening over the quiet Chinnereth.[1]

Deborah was there at Barak's request—rather, his demand. Through her, the Lord had called Barak to lead the attack on Sisera. But he had refused unless she agreed to come up with him from Ramah. She did, but his insistence grieved her.

Young military runners kept Deborah informed on the battle's progress, but she already knew it was a rout. That morning from Mount Tabor she watched Barak's two divisions sweep

---

[1] The Sea of Chinnereth was later called the Sea of Galilee and the Sea of Tiberius. Today it is also referred to as the Sea of Kinneret.

around the mountain's north and south, crunching down on the flanks of Sisera's proud chariots like a lion's jaw. The Canaanite warriors panicked and fled back west through the Jezreel valley, only to trap themselves against the rain-swollen Kishon River. The voracious Israelites leaped on them with a vengeance and consumed what was left of Sisera's army.

En route back to Kedesh, Deborah heard that Sisera escaped. Barak was hot on his trail, but she knew Barak wouldn't catch him.

Dusk was falling when the last runner shouted, "Victory is complete! Sisera is dead! Barak and his men are nearing town!" Deborah overflowed in thankful prayer as she went to meet Barak. Just outside the village she saw the small warrior contingent approaching with the slow pride of victorious fatigue.

"The Lord be praised, Deborah!" shouted Barak, from about fifty feet away. "He has done just as he said! Sisera fell into my hands, and the Canaanite yoke on Israel is broken!" Victory cries erupted from soldiers and the gathering crowd. Women danced their joy with tambourines.

Deborah shouted back, "Yes, Barak! Praise the Glory of Israel who has kept his word and strengthened your hand and the hands of every valiant one who fought Sisera and his boastful host!" Another celebratory roar broke out, followed by more dancing and singing.

As the throng reveled, Barak and Deborah pulled away for a full battle report. They sat near the fire outside Barak's house, and he savored a large helping of his wife's roasted lamb.

"Who was she?" Deborah asked.

He knew immediately what she meant. Sisera's army had fallen into Barak's hands, but Sisera had not. Sisera had fallen into a woman's hands, just as Deborah had predicted.

"Jael, the wife of Heber the Kenite," he answered, still chewing. "Her tent isn't even four miles from here."

"Tell me what happened," said Deborah.

"Jael was brilliant. She spied Sisera trying to escape unnoticed, and persuaded him to hide in her tent. When he learned she was a Kenite, he assumed she was an ally. She hid him in the storage trough in her floor, covered him with a rug, and gave him some milk. Weary and warm, he fell asleep like a baby. When she took me in, he was still lying there—with a tent peg through his brain! She had driven it through his temple with a hammer!" He shook his head and took a gulp of wine. Wiping his beard, he said, "That woman showed more courage than most of my warriors."

"The Lord be praised for Jael's courage. Her glory will be sung for many generations," Deborah said. "But that glory should have been yours, Barak."

Barak poured some more wine. Then cradling the cup in both hands, he stared into the fire. "I still don't understand what evil I committed in wanting you to come with me. You're a prophetess. Who wouldn't want a prophet of the Lord with him when going into battle?"

"Wanting a prophet with you wasn't evil," replied Deborah. "The evil was refusing to go to battle *unless* I went with you." Barak's brow furrowed. "Barak," she said earnestly. He looked over at her. "It was the Lord who promised that he would give Sisera into your hand. My role as a prophet was just to speak the Lord's word to you. The power lay in the promise, not the prophet. When you refused to go unless I accompanied you, it revealed that your confidence was in me, not in God's word. By trusting my presence for victory more than God's promise, you gave the messenger more glory than the message. It made me an idol. *That* was the evil. God kept his promise to you because he is always faithful. But because you took glory away from him and gave it to another, he took glory away from you and gave it to another."

○○

The writer of Hebrews says, "Remember your leaders, those who spoke to you the word of God. Consider the outcome of their way of life, and imitate their faith" (Heb. 13:7).

Imitating the faith of godly leaders is a biblical command. We obey and submit to them because they are faithful (Heb. 13:17). They trust God, obey his Word, and take great care to speak the truth to us accurately. We should want to be just like that.

But when, like Barak, we become more dependent on our leaders, or our association with them, than on God's promises to us, we turn leaders into idols. We cease to imitate their faith and instead make them an object of our faith. Our idolatry robs God of glory that only he deserves and gives it to another, something God won't abide (Isa. 48:11). But our idolatry also robs us of the only solid Rock that can support the house of our faith. Idolizing our leaders is building our faith-house on sand (Matt. 7:24–27). God is merciful to discipline us when we do this.

Barak was a man of faith, and he faithfully obeyed God's Word (Heb. 11:32). Let us imitate him in the *action* of his faith, but let us differ from him in the *object* of our faith. Our faith should not be in our godly leaders' faith, but rather in the Object of their faith. Let us imitate, not idolize, their faith.

"This Book of the Law shall not depart from your mouth, but you shall meditate on it day and night, so that you may be careful to do according to all that is written in it. For then you will make your way prosperous, and then you will have good success. Have I not commanded you? Be strong and courageous. Do not be frightened, and do not be dismayed, for the LORD your God is with you wherever you go."

JOSHUA 1:8-9

27

WHEN FEAR ATTACKS

JOSHUA AND COURAGE

Joshua

REGARDLESS OF OUR SITUATION, following Jesus requires all of us to repeatedly exercise courage. The Lord frequently calls us to face or do things we're afraid of, and Joshua, the son of Nun, is an example for us. His call was to lead Israel in battle after battle, decade after decade, facing strong army after strong army in order to occupy the land the Lord had promised. Through the imagined reminiscence of one of Joshua's soldiers, let's ponder what it means to learn the life-long habit of exercising "strong and courageous" faith (Josh. 1:9).

○○

"Here we are," said Amattai, as he and his seventeen-year-old son Levi approached the simply but lovingly carved exterior of the tomb-cave holding the remains of Joshua the son of Nun, Moses's successor and Israel's beloved general-in-chief.

Early that morning, they had departed their home in Janohah, nestled in the northwestern hills of Ephraim, and made the twenty-five mile hike to Joshua's city of Timnath-serah. Levi, now taller than his father, looked very much a man, except for the wispy, premature beard. It would not be long before he would enlist in Israel's army. Amattai planned this pilgrimage as part of his son's preparation.

The nine-hour walk had flown by, father and son engrossed in the verbal history of Israel's great victories under Joshua over the thirty-one kings of Canaan. They dissected strategy, tactics, geography, topography, weaponry, and feats of faith, force, and failure. Amattai was a mine of fascinating stories and military facts. His father, Chiliab, had fought in many of the battles, and served under Joshua for twenty-one years, until a fever took him at forty-one—the age Amattai was now. Amattai himself had fought in the last few battles, when Joshua was a very old man.

Standing at the great man's grave, the father asked, "Can you remember meeting Joshua?"

"A little," said Levi. "I don't really remember his face. I remember him being old and putting his hand on my head and saying something to me. I remember feeling scared of him, and you telling me to stand up straight!"

Amattai smiled. "You were only four or five. He died when you were six."

"What do you remember most about Joshua?" asked Levi.

Amattai thought, as he pulled up some grass that had taken root near the tomb's stone, careful not to touch the grave itself. "He was the most humble and the most courageous man I've ever known," replied Amattai. "His humility made him ruthlessly honest about himself. I was amazed at how plainly he talked about his fears and sins, what most men try to hide from each other."

"Fears? I thought Joshua was fearless," said Levi, surprised.

"Well, he seemed fearless because he was so courageous. But he taught me a lesson about fear and courage that I've never forgotten.

"I had only been with the army a few weeks and hadn't seen any real fighting yet. Six or seven of us untested warriors were sitting around a fire one evening talking about the impending battle against Aphek. We were all blowing a lot of brave-sounding hot air because none of us wanted to look like a coward, though inside we were all plenty scared.

"Suddenly Joshua stepped into the firelight. We all jumped up, hoping he hadn't overheard our foolish talk. He had. He said to us, 'So, none of you young men are afraid to fight Aphek?' We all glanced at each other and shook our heads— lying. Then he said, 'Well, you're all better men than I am. I frequently have to face down fear, even after all these years.'" Hearing this shook us a bit. We all believed Joshua feared nothing.

"I can still see him staring into the fire and saying, 'I'll tell you when fear hits me. When I see a strong king and his army arrayed against us, with hundreds of swift chariots and a forest of spears. In that moment, the Lord's promises seem to drain out of my memory and I start thinking that this battle is up to me. That's when the doubts attack. I can doubt my judgment. I can doubt our strategy, our weapons, our timing, and our numbers. I remember how Moses led us, and I can doubt my ability to lead. At that point, fear becomes my most dangerous enemy. The fear is paralyzing.'

"Then he looked up at us and said, 'That's why the Lord has had to tell me many times to "be strong and courageous."[1] He knows the fears I'm vulnerable to. And what I've learned is this: it requires real strength both to remember what the Lord has promised to do for us and to move my trust off myself and back on him. And it requires real courage to act on what the Lord's promises tell me and not what my doubting fears tell me. It takes *strength* to trust the Lord and *courage* to obey him.'

"And when Joshua turned to leave, he said to us, 'You

---

[1] Seven times in Deuteronomy 31 and Joshua 1, Joshua was exhorted to be "strong and courageous."

men may not struggle like me. But someday it may help to remember that courage is often not the absence of fear but the conquering of it.'

"I can tell you, Levi, Joshua's words have helped me conquer a thousand fears," Amattai said. Then, reaching over and placing an affectionate hand on the back of Levi's neck, he said, "Son, that's the strength and courage you'll need, no matter what battle you're fighting."

○ ○

Our progress in becoming like Jesus (Rom. 8:29), as well as our progress in building his kingdom, is often slow and difficult, much like Israel's taking of the Promised Land. Each battle and each foe is different. If we learn not to fear one foe, it's no guarantee that we won't have to overcome fear when facing another. And some foes will always stir up fear in us. Each encounter calls for new strength and courage.

But fear doesn't have to discourage us; it is the Lord's design. Facing our fear tests our faith, and faith is what pleases God (Heb. 11:6). God desires that we grow strong in faith (Rom. 4:20), and the "constant practice" of exercising faith produces strong, mature faith in us (Heb. 5:14). So it should not surprise us that God frequently tests our faith by making us face things we fear (1 Pet. 4:12; James 1:3).

So when fear attacks, rather than surrendering or fleeing from it, let it remind us that our call is to conquer fear—no, more than conquer it through him who loved us (Rom. 8:37). When we are forced to repeatedly be "strong and courageous" (Josh. 1:9), it teaches us the habit of mustering the strength to remember God's promises, and the courage to act in faith. It is through faith that we learn not to fear anything that is frightening (1 Pet. 3:6).

Fear is a call to exercise faith. So we can stop dreading fear. Instead, we can see fear as another means God is using to fulfill his promise to complete the good work he began in us (Phil. 1:6).

Now the Syrians on one of their raids had carried off a little girl from the land of Israel, and she worked in the service of Naaman's wife.

2 KINGS 5:2

28

GOD MAKES OUR MISERY THE SERVANT OF HIS MERCY

NAAMAN, THE SERVANT GIRL, AND SOVEREIGN MERCY

Based on 2 Kings 5:1–19

NAAMAN WAS SYRIA'S FOREMOST general when Elisha served as God's foremost prophet in Israel. After a Syrian raid on Israel, Naaman brought back his wife a gift: a Hebrew servant girl. When this servant girl saw that Naaman suffered from a serious leprous skin disease, she told Naaman about Elisha and the power of Yahweh. As a result, Naaman was healed.

In this story, God's miraculous power is clearly seen in Naaman's healing. But in the background stands the servant girl. And in her we see God's power to make our misery the servant of his mercy.

○○

"The master's returned! The master's returned!" Shamura and her servant girl, Anyroda, were laying out fabric on the table when they heard the servant boy shouting outside.[1]

---

[1] The names of Naaman's wife and her Hebrew servant girl are fictional.

Shamura dropped the fabric and hurried out to greet her husband. Anyroda stayed behind, busying herself with the fabric. But what she was really doing was avoiding her master.

As Shamura stepped outside, Naaman stepped out of his chariot and strode quickly toward her. She could tell he was excited, but trying to hide it. The news must be good, she thought. She walked to meet him, smiling, and he kissed her and embraced her tightly. "You are a sweet sight for longing eyes," he said.

Shamura stepped back and said, "Well?"

Naaman pulled up the left sleeve of his robe, exposing his upper arm where one of the diseased spots had been. The skin was healthy and soft. "No spots anywhere," he announced. "I am a leper no more."

Shamura cupped her mouth and her eyes teared. Then she said softly, "The gods be praised!"

Naaman put his arm around Shamura's shoulder, and they began walking slowly toward the house. "No," he said softly. "The 'gods,' at least as we've understood them, had nothing to do with this. Rimmon was powerless to cure my disease. I was healed by Yahweh."

Shamura could tell by Naaman's tone that more than just his skin was changed.

"Where is Anyroda?" Naaman asked.

Shamura glanced around but didn't see her. "She must still be in the house. We were preparing fabric for a new robe when you arrived."

"I need to speak with her," said Naaman. He clapped his hands twice, which brought his young servant boy running. "Send for Anyroda. She's in the house," Naaman instructed. The boy was off.

A minute later Anyroda stepped out the door apprehensively.

"Anyroda, come! You have nothing to fear. It worked!" Anyroda had never seen Naaman smile like that. She straightened and her eyes widened. She walked over to them.

"I have something to show you," said Naaman, and he pulled up his sleeve to reveal his healed skin.

"You're healed?" Anyroda asked breathlessly.

"Yes," he replied, "completely healed by Yahweh, your God—and now mine. And I would never have been healed or ever known the true God if you hadn't told me about your prophet. Anyroda, I owe you more than I could ever hope to repay."

Anyroda's eyes dropped to the ground. Her master, one of Syria's greatest men, had barely acknowledged her prior to this trip. The respect she now felt from him was hard to absorb.

"What is your Hebrew name? I've never asked," said Naaman.

"Miriam," she answered.

"What does it mean?"

"It's the name of a great prophetess, but in Hebrew it means *bitter*."

"Bitter," said Naaman, more to himself than to her. "That's fitting." He was quiet for a moment, and then said, "May we call you Miriam?"

Miriam nodded.

"I thought of you many times, Miriam, on our journey back, riding through your homeland. I had never noticed how beautiful it was before. I suppose it is more beautiful to me now that I know it is the land of the true God."

Miriam bowed her head and wiped tears from her eyes.

Naaman held out his hand and said, "Come, Miriam, I have something else to show you." Miriam dried her hand and took Naaman's. He led her behind the horses where two mules stood, each carrying two large baskets of dirt.

"These baskets hold earth from Israel, near the great prophet's house. Never again will I sacrifice to any other god but Yahweh, for now I know that there is no other. And when I offer sacrifice, it will be on the soil Yahweh promised to give to his people—to *your* people.

"Miriam, I see now that I have been the source of great bitterness for you. I stole you away from your family, from your people, and from Yahweh's land. All this time I assumed that I had done *you* a great favor, bringing you to a great kingdom to serve in the house of a great general. I thought I was giving you a life you would never have had otherwise. But I was a fool. I am the one who received the great favor."

Tears filled the strong man's eyes, and he said with difficulty, "Yahweh sent you to point me to him. I would never have known him, had you not come to my house. Because of you, Miriam, Yahweh has given me a life I would never have had otherwise."

Master and servant wept together.

○○

Naaman's story is more than a story of God's sovereign power over disease. It's more than a story of God's sovereign grace extended to the nations and to his enemies. It is also a glorious story of God's sovereign mercy conquering human evil and heartbreak.

The Syrians abducted a Hebrew girl from her family. It was a wicked sin. The girl, her parents, and her siblings experienced a nightmare of misery from which they could never wake. It left them traumatized and scarred. They wept for grief and pleaded with God for mercy.

And God answered. But he did not answer by returning the girl home (unless Naaman later freed her). God answered by using her to give Naaman the mercy of healing and saving faith. God used her to give the Syrian people the mercy of seeing his reality and glory. And God used this displaced servant girl to preserve a testimony of his mercy toward undeserving sinners that has been retold to billions of people for thousands of years.

Behind all the great manifestations of God's mighty mercy in history are stories of great misery. Do not miss the action in the background. It's there to fuel your faith. God will overpower every evil you will experience in this life and make you more than a conqueror through Christ who loved you (Rom. 8:37).

The evil that causes your greatest misery will one day serve the omnipotent mercy of God, not only for you, but also for more people than you ever imagined.

A dispute also arose among them, as to which of them was to be regarded as the greatest.

LUKE 22:24

29

ESCAPING THE SUICIDAL SLAVERY OF SELFISH AMBITION

THE DISCIPLES AND SELFISH AMBITION

Luke 22:14–30

SELFISH AMBITION IS A sin that always seems to be "crouching at the door" (Gen. 4:7). It contaminates our motives for doing just about anything. It shows up even in the most holy moments, like it did for Jesus's disciples in Luke's account of the Last Supper (Luke 22:14–30). But in that account we also see how Jesus frees us from the suicidal slavery of selfish ambition.

○ ○

Jesus's final meal before he went to the cross was perhaps the most ironic time for the Twelve to debate over which of them was the greatest.

The greatest human being who ever walked the earth, the Founder and Perfecter of their faith (Heb. 12:2), was reclining at the table with them. He was the only one in the room without sin (Heb. 4:15). He was the only one there who always did what was pleasing to the Father (John 8:29).

This person had just led the Twelve through the last Passover meal before his death—the death that would be the propitiating sacrifice for *their* sins (Rom. 3:25). As Jesus broke bread with the disciples, he instituted the new Passover meal, which they and all future disciples were to observe regularly until he returned so that they would always remember that their sins were forgiven only through the substitutionary, atoning death of the true Passover Lamb (Acts 10:43).

This was no time for any disciple to assert his own greatness, except the greatness of his sin.

Facing their sin, ironically, is what ignited the disciples' "greatness" debate.

Jesus had just revealed that one of them that very night would willingly participate in the most spectacular sin in history: the slaughter of the Son of God.[1] Yet somehow, the introspection and inquiry that followed ended up in a competition over who was greatest (Matt. 26:22).

It was a moment that displayed the terrifying and blinding power of pride in sinful people. Jesus was about to die *for their sins*. One of them was about to betray him to that death. Their response to such horror and glory should have been mourning, repentance, and worship. Instead, each disciple was suddenly and absurdly preoccupied with his own place of prominence. How quickly the moon of selfish ambition eclipses the Sun of Righteousness (Mal. 4:2).

But where sin increased, Jesus's grace abounded all the more (Rom. 5:20). The disciples' pride, along with all their sins, would be paid in full. Therefore, Jesus did not condemn his disciples for thinking far too highly of themselves (Rom. 12:3) at the worst possible time.

Instead, Jesus mercifully drew their gaze off of themselves and back to him:

> The kings of the Gentiles exercise lordship over them, and those in authority over them are called benefactors. But not

---

[1] See John Piper, *Spectacular Sins* (Wheaton, IL: Crossway, 2008), 98.

so with you. Rather, let the greatest among you become as the youngest, and the leader as one who serves. For who is the greater, one who reclines at table or one who serves? Is it not the one who reclines at table? But I am among you as the one who serves. (Luke 22:25–26)

○ ○

God reminds us of his mercy through Luke's account of the disciples' sin, because we, too, are frequently tempted to sin in this way, even in the most sacred moments.

When we display sinful pride and comparison, we know that our attention is in the wrong place. When we begin to compare and compete, our selfish focus leads us into a black hole of demonic jealousy (James 3:14–15). But looking to Jesus (Heb. 12:2) reminds us that we have nothing that we haven't received through him (1 Cor. 4:7). Past and future, world without end, all is God's grace toward us in Christ. Looking to Jesus reminds us that loving and serving each other, just as Jesus loves and serves us, is the path to full joy (John 15:11–12).

We will have to fight against selfish ambition as long as we live, because it's right at the core of our fallen nature. Our sinful hearts desire to be like God (Gen. 3:5) and pursue others' worship. We don't need to feign shock when we see selfishness in ourselves and, like Jesus, we should be patient when we see it in others.

Looking away from ourselves to Jesus is the key to walking in joyful freedom from selfish ambition. God designed us to be satisfied with Jesus's glory, not our own.

Mary therefore took a pound of expensive ointment made from pure nard, and anointed the feet of Jesus and wiped his feet with her hair.

JOHN 12:3

30

WHEN WASTING YOUR LIFE IS WORSHIP

JUDAS, MARY, AND WORSHIP

John 12:1–8

WE ALL ARE HAPPINESS hunters. We are all treasure seekers. And as Judas and Mary illustrate, there's one sure way to measure what we treasure: what we're willing to spend to obtain it.

○○

The dinner table was buzzing with happy conversation. As Lazarus fielded a stream of questions about what it was like to die, and Martha cleared empty plates and filled empty wine bowls, Mary quietly slipped away into another room.

When she returned, she carried a large wooden bowl with a small alabaster jar inside. She knelt down near Jesus's feet, placed the bowl on the floor, and removed her headdress. The talking trailed away as Jesus turned toward her and sat up. Soon everyone was straining or standing to get a better look at what she was doing.

Mary removed the small jar and then reverently placed Jesus's feet inside the bowl. She picked up the jar, removed the stopper, and poured its contents slowly on Jesus's feet. The room was wordless as she gathered her long hair in her right hand and used it to wipe Jesus's feet. An exotic, breathtaking fragrance wafted across the room. The guests exchanged wide-eyed glances. Everyone knew this was a rare perfume.

Jesus was moved. His eyes were full of intense affection as he watched Mary work.

Judas was moved too, but not with affection. He was irritated. He simply could not fathom Mary's wasteful extravagance. That perfume had to have been worth nearly a year's wages. Never once in three years had Jesus's disciples had that amount of money at one time. And there it sat, contaminated, a worthless puddle in a bowl.

His indignant objection shot through the silence: "Why was this ointment not sold for three hundred denarii and given to the poor?"[1]

This question tensed the atmosphere. Mary stopped and looked sadly at the floor. All other eyes turned to Jesus. To a number of the disciples, this seemed like a fair question. Jesus typically instructed them to give any extra money in their collective moneybag to the needy. Often "extra" meant beyond what they needed that day. Mary's act did seem a bit indulgent.

Jesus said nothing for a moment and continued to stare at Mary. He knew what they were all thinking. And he knew that Judas had questioned her "not because he cared about the poor, but because he was a thief, and having charge of the moneybag he used to help himself to what was put into it." Judas's noble-sounding protest was no more than a disguise for his greed. Jesus grieved over Judas's duplicity and how he contaminated Mary's worship.

Then Jesus said, "Leave her alone, so that she make keep it for the day of my burial. For the poor you always have with

---

[1] The quotations in this story are from John 12:5–8.

you," turning his piercing eyes to Judas with potent sorrow, "but you do not always have me."

○ ○

Judas and Mary are contrasts in treasuring. They both had hedonistic motives; neither acted out of stoic duty. Both pursued the treasure they believed would make them happy. To Mary, Jesus was the priceless Pearl (Matt. 13:45), whom she loved more than anything and spent what was likely her greatest earthly possession to honor. To Judas, thirty pieces of silver was a fair price for the Pearl.

Judas's sin wasn't that he was hunting happiness. His sin was believing that money would make him happier than Christ.

O Judas, the tragedy of your miscalculation! The Pearl, worth more than the entire universe, sat in front of you and all you could see were puddles of perfume. You grieved the squandering of a year's wages while you squandered infinite, eternal Treasure!

Jesus leads all his disciples to watershed moments when the choices we make, not the words we say, reveal the treasure we want. These moments are designed to make us count this cost: "Whoever loves his life loses it, and whoever hates his life in this world will keep it for eternal life" (John 12:25). These moments force us to choose what we really believe is gain, whether we value the Pearl or puddles.

If we choose the Pearl, we hear in Judas's objection the world's appraisal of us. They watch as we pour our valuable time, intellect, money, youth, financial future, and vocation out on Jesus's feet. They watch them puddle in the bowls of churches, mission fields, orphanages, and homes where children are raised and careers are lost. And what they see is foolish waste. We hear their rebuke, not their respect.

Jesus wants you to waste your life like Mary wasted her perfume. For it is no true waste. It is true worship. A poured-out life of love for Jesus that counts worldly gain as loss displays how precious he really is. It preaches to a bewildered, disdainful world that Christ is gain and the real waste is gaining the world's perfume while losing one's soul (Matt. 16:26).

Are you wasting your life?

[Judas] was a thief, and having charge of the moneybag he used to help himself to what was put into it.

JOHN 12:6

31

JUDAS CARRIED THE MONEYBAG?

JUDAS AND THE LOVE OF MONEY

John 12:6

JESUS PUT A THIEF in charge of his moneybag. Has that ever struck you as odd?

Jesus could have given the moneybag to Nathanael, "an Israelite indeed, in whom there [was] no deceit" (John 1:47), or to John, "the disciple whom Jesus loved" (John 21:20), or to Levi, who had extensive financial experience (Luke 5:27). But he didn't. Jesus chose Judas to be the treasurer of his itinerant nonprofit.

One is tempted to offer the Lord some consulting on good stewardship. Donors were financially supporting this ministry (Luke 8:3), and Jesus appointed the one guy he knew was a "devil" (John 6:70) to manage the money. But this was not poor judgment on Jesus's part. It was deliberate. He knew Judas was pilfering. Why did Jesus allow it?

I believe Jesus was putting his money where his mouth was.

Jesus had said, "Do not lay up for yourselves treasures on earth, where . . . thieves break in and steal" (Matt. 6:19–20). In letting Judas carry the moneybag, Jesus showed us by example what he meant.

Jesus said, "Where your treasure is, there your heart will be also" (Matt. 6:21). In Judas, Jesus showed us the heart-hardening, heart-blinding, heartbreaking end of treasuring the wrong thing.

And Jesus had said, "No one can serve two masters, for either he will hate the one and love the other, or he will be devoted to the one and despise the other. You cannot serve God and money" (Matt. 6:24). In Judas, Jesus showed us an alarming example of what loving money and hating God can look like.

Shockingly, for quite a while loving money and hating God can actually look to others like devotion to God. This is what is unnerving about Judas.

For a long time, Judas's reputation was as a student and close companion of Jesus. Judas lived with Jesus and the other eleven disciples for the better part of three years. He traveled long, dusty roads with these missionary comrades. He ate with them, sat around evening fires with them talking about the kingdom of God, and prayed with them. He heard more of Jesus's sermons than almost anybody. He received personal instruction from Jesus. He witnessed Jesus's incredible miracles and saw the Father provide for their needs over and over again.

All during the time Judas was part of the Twelve, he mostly said and outwardly performed the right things. It's astonishing that none of Judas's fellow disciples perceived his deceitfulness. Even when Jesus finally sent Judas off to carry out his betrayal, the others didn't seem to suspect him (John 13:28–29). It was a stunning and grievous blow to them all when in the end he sold Jesus for thirty pieces of silver (Matt. 26:15).

Judas's masquerade is a lesson for us. Wolves can look and sound almost exactly like sheep. And sometimes Jesus, for his own reasons, allows the disguised wolves to live among the sheep for a long time and do great damage before their deception is exposed. When this happens, we must trust that the Lord knows what he's doing. Judas reminds us that even ravaging wolves have a part to play in the drama of redemptive history.

But in knowingly giving dishonest Judas the moneybag, Jesus specifically modeled for us where *not* to put our trust: money. Jesus trusted his Father, not money, to provide everything he needed to fulfill his calling. He slept in peace every night, knowing that Judas was embezzling.

Judas, on the other hand, became the archetypal model of 1 Timothy 6:10: "For the love of money is a root of all kinds of evils. It is through this craving that some have wandered away from the faith and pierced themselves with many pangs." In Judas's example, Jesus warns us that the love of money can be so deceptive that we can wander to the point where we are willing to sell eternal Treasure for a handful of coins. The seductive power of wealth must make us tremble.

Not all parts of this story have direct application for us. Jesus doesn't intend for us to follow his example in appointing thieves as treasurers. Only God is wise enough to do that.

But Jesus does intend for us to follow his example in knowingly seeking the kingdom first, believing that all we need will be given to us by our Father (Matt. 6:33). His word to us is "fear not, little flock, for it is your Father's good pleasure to give you the kingdom" (Luke 12:32). Our Father can easily out-give what any thief can steal.

"If anyone would come after me, let him deny himself and take up his cross and follow me."

MARK 8:34

32

IF YOU WANT TO BE HAPPY, YOU MUST DENY YOURSELF

THE DISCIPLES AND SELF-DENIAL

Mark 8:34–38

THE CHRISTIAN LIFE IS a journey to the greatest joy that exists. But "the way is hard that leads to life, and those who find it are few" (Matt. 7:14). Why is that? Because, paradoxically, in order to pursue our greatest joy, we must deny ourselves.

○○

It was a moment of euphoria for the disciples. Jesus *was* the Christ. Peter had confessed it and Jesus had confirmed it. The long-awaited arrival of Israel's Messiah had come! And the Twelve relished their place alongside him.

Then, oddly, Jesus started talking about suffering many things, and being murdered by his enemies, and rising again from the dead. The disciples were confused: how could defeat be the path to the Christ's glory? The Christ was to be victorious.

So Peter brought correction to Jesus, and Jesus called his correction satanic. Peter was stunned. What could be satanic about wanting the Christ to be victorious? Jesus's answer was, "You are not setting your mind on the things of God, but on the things of man" (Mark 8:33).

Jesus knew that all the disciples, as well as the crowd following him, were thinking the same thing. So he gathered
them all together and let go with one more wrecking ball to
their worldview: "If anyone would come after me, let him deny
himself and take up his cross and follow me" (Mark 8:34).

The crowd stilled, a sea of bewildered faces. A cross? They
all knew what that meant: Roman execution of the most hor-
rific, fearful kind. They were all hoping that Jesus would conquer their enemies, free them from such tyranny, and "restore
the kingdom to Israel" (Acts 1:6). Carrying a Roman cross did
not sound like the messianic kingdom they were longing for.
It sounded like death. Jesus wanted them to die?

Yes.

Jesus's kingdom was not of this world—not of the geo-
political world that these first followers knew (John 18:36).
His kingdom was far broader in scope than any of them yet
realized. And their true enemy was far more powerful and
deadly than Rome. Rome was a drop in the bucket (Isa. 40:15).
Their real enemy dwelled in them and all around them. Jesus
had indeed come to conquer that enemy. In just a few days, he
would head to Jerusalem to strike the decisive blow.

So now Jesus was preparing them for the cross—his first
and foremost, then theirs—and the multimillennial mission
to call out true Israel from all peoples into his kingdom. Jesus
was teaching them to intentionally move toward death.

All present that day would die physically, some as martyrs.
But all his followers would also have to die spiritually, to themselves. They would have to die to the desire for self-glory, die
to the desire for worldly respect, die to the fear of man, die to
the desire for an easy life, die to the desire for earthly wealth,
and die a thousand other deaths. Finally, they would have to
die to their desire to save their earthly lives.

But Jesus wasn't calling his followers to some stoic life of self-sacrifice. He was inviting them to joy beyond their imagination. The broad road of the world was lined with seductive false promises, appealing to and blinding sinful human heart-eyes and leading many to a horror beyond imagination. So Jesus was calling his followers to deny themselves the world's paltry, brief joys so that they might have overflowing eternal joy. He was calling them to deny themselves hell, that they might take up heaven.

> For whoever would save his life will lose it, but whoever loses his life for my sake and the gospel's will save it. For what does it profit a man to gain the whole world and forfeit his soul? For what can a man give in return for his soul? For whoever is ashamed of me and of my words in this adulterous and sinful generation, of him will the Son of Man also be ashamed when he comes in the glory of his Father with the holy angels. (Mark 8:35–38)

○ ○

The Christian life is hard, sometimes agonizing, but we shouldn't be surprised (1 Pet. 4:12). The Christian life is hard because denying our fallen selves is hard. Our lives are our most precious earthly possession. Nothing displays the worth of Jesus more than our willingness to give away our lives (in small and large ways) for his sake.

Years ago, in a lullaby I wrote for my oldest daughter, I tried to capture, for her and for me, the heavenly logic of this paradoxical pursuit of joy:

> There's joy beyond your wildest dreams if you will just
> believe:
> This aching thirst for joy you feel God only can relieve,
> And that eternal life is what's in store
> For all who will believe that only he's worth living for.

The only things that Jesus asks us to deny are what will rob us of eternal joy. Like Moses in Hebrews 11:25–26, we are called to deny ourselves the passing pleasures of sin and consider the reproach of Christ greater wealth than the world's treasures. How? By looking to the reward!

"Lord, what about this man?"

JOHN 21:21

33

JESUS WANTS YOU TO BE YOU

PETER AND CALLING

John 21:15–23

GOD HAD *YOU SPECIFICALLY* in mind when he created you and called you to follow him. You are custom-designed for your calling. But when you face the difficulty of your calling, you may look at others and be tempted to wonder why they don't seem to bear the same burdens you do. The apostle Peter faced the same temptation.

○○

After the resurrected Jesus served his sleep-deprived fishermen-disciples a seaside breakfast of miracle fish, he took Peter on a walk down the beach. Jesus wanted to tell Peter a few important things directly before Jesus parted physically from him for the last time in this age. John trailed them, about ten yards behind.

Toward the end of their conversation, Jesus dropped a bombshell on Peter: "Truly, truly, I say to you, when you were young, you used to dress yourself and walk wherever you wanted, but when you are old, you will stretch out your hands, and another will dress you and carry you where you do not want to go."[1] Then Jesus, as only he could do, peered right into Peter's soul and said, "Follow me."

Peter had already been dreading Jesus's final departure, wondering how this small, fearful band of disciples would survive without him. Peter wondered how *he* would survive. Now Jesus informed him that he wasn't going to survive. Peter was going to die for Jesus. Only this time Peter issued no overconfident proclamation like he had during the Passover meal. Now he knew how weak he really was. Left to himself, he was a coward.

But Peter remembered that he would not be left to himself like an orphan; Jesus, though gone, would somehow come to him in the future (John 14:18). Peter believed this. Jesus had never once failed to keep a promise. But how Jesus would come to him at the moment of his execution, Peter could not conceive. He already felt lonely.

And Peter wondered why Jesus hadn't spoken of other disciples' deaths. Was he the only one who would have to die? Peter looked around for the others and he saw John, who was walking just where the cool surf gently pushed up and bathed his feet. Peter knew how Jesus loved John, and he wondered if Jesus was going to spare John the cost that he was asking Peter to pay. Gesturing back, Peter asked Jesus, "Lord, what about this man?"

Jesus's brow furrowed as he watched two gulls quarrel over a dead fish. Then he looked at Peter and responded with his familiar tender firmness, "If it is my will that he remain until I come, what is that to you? You follow me!"

○○

Jesus calls each one of us to follow him (John 15:16). All of God's promises are yes to each one of us in Christ (2 Cor.

---

[1] The quotations in this story are from John 21:18–23.

1:20). We each get to share in Christ's inheritance (Col. 1:12), and as members of Christ's united body we need each other (Rom. 12:5).

But we do not all have the same function (Rom. 12:4). Each disciple, each individual member of the body, has a unique role. And each must lead the life that the Lord has assigned to him, and to which God has called him (1 Cor. 7:17).

The question, "What is that to you?" is one you and I need to ask frequently. How God deals with other people is often of excessive concern to us, especially if their paths don't seem to be paved with the same pain as ours.

The fallen part of our nature doesn't look at others and glory in how each of them uniquely bears the *imago dei* (Gen. 1:27). It doesn't revel in others' distinctive refraction of God's multifaceted glory. It doesn't rejoice in the sweet providences God grants to them. It is not grateful for the blessings of their God-given strengths. It does not want to deal gently with their weaknesses (Heb. 5:2). Full of pride and selfish ambition, our fallen nature uses others to gauge our own significance, how successful and impressive we perceive ourselves to be.

But there is gospel in Jesus's words: "What is that to you? You follow me!" Do you hear it? It's a declaration of liberation. Jesus died to make you "free indeed" (John 8:36), and this includes freedom from the tyranny of sinful comparison and coveting another's calling.

God had *you* in mind when he created you (Ps. 139:13–16). He knew just what he was doing. You, your body, your mind, and your circumstances are not an accident. Yes, he's aware of your deficiencies, and, yes, he's calling you to grow in grace (2 Pet. 3:18). But God does not expect or intend you to be someone else. Nor does he want you to follow someone else's path.

Jesus wants you to be *you*. The faith that Jesus gives you is sufficient for the path he gives you (Rom. 12:3). And the grace he gives you to face your trials will be sufficient for you when the need comes (2 Cor. 12:9).

You are your truest you not when you are analyzing yourself or measuring yourself against someone else. You are your truest you when your eyes are fixed on Jesus (Heb. 12:2), when you are following him in faith, and when you are serving others in love with the grace-gifts God has assigned to you (Rom. 12:4–8).

So, no matter what today holds, be free from saying in your heart, "Lord what about this man?" For Jesus *chose* you (John 15:16), promised to supply all that you need (Phil. 4:19), and wants you to simply follow him.

If you humble yourself under his mighty hand, trusting him to redeem all your suffering, "thorns" (2 Cor. 12:7), and weaknesses, he will exalt you at the time and in the way that will bring him the most glory and you the most joy (1 Pet. 5:6).

"He will wipe away every tear from their eyes, and death shall be no more, neither shall there be mourning, nor crying, nor pain anymore, for the former things have passed away."

REVELATION 21:4

34

THE TREASURE MAKES ALL THE DIFFERENCE

THE MAN WHO FOUND THE TREASURE AND THE RESURRECTION

Matthew 13:44

ONE OF JESUS'S MOST powerful parables is also one of his shortest:

> The kingdom of heaven is like a treasure hidden in a field, which a man found and covered up. Then in his joy he goes and sells all that he has and buys that field. (Matt. 13:44)

Fifteen minutes before this man's discovery in the field, the thought of selling all that he owned to buy it wouldn't have crossed his mind. Even if it had, it would have seemed ludicrous. But fifteen minutes after finding the treasure, he was off to do it with joy. What made the difference?

The treasure.

This man suddenly found something that transformed his whole outlook on life. The treasure restructured his values and priorities. It altered his goals. The treasure revolutionized the man.

The treasure in this parable is the resurrection to eternal life. It was the same "treasure in heaven" that Jesus promised the rich young man if he would sell his possessions, give to the poor, and follow Jesus (Matt. 19:21). The rich young man, blinded by short-term worldly wealth, could not see the treasure, but the man in the parable did, and he jumped at it.

Now, there was a cost to obtaining the treasure. Viewed one way, the cost seemed high—it cost him everything he owned. But viewed another way, the cost was very small. Standing in the field, the man did a quick cost-benefit analysis. It didn't take him long to realize that selling all his possessions was going to make him wealthy beyond his wildest dreams. He would have been a fool not to do whatever was necessary to buy that field.

When the man bought the field and obtained the treasure of eternal life, what specifically did he get? This is an important question, because the Bible makes eternal life a central focus for the Christian—yet it provides few descriptions about what it will be like. When the Bible does describe eternal life, it often uses similes, metaphors, and symbols. Why?

One reason is that we simply are not yet equipped to comprehend the reality we will experience in the new age, for "no eye has seen, nor ear heard, nor the heart of man imagined, what God has prepared for those who love him" (1 Cor. 2:9). Through figurative language, God helps us transpose the glories we now see and understand into glimpses of future greater glories.

But I believe there is a more important reason God doesn't give us more details: eternal life is more about a Person than a place. What will make the kingdom of heaven so heavenly to us will not be the glorious phenomena of the new creation or the rich rewards we will receive, as inexpressibly wonderful as they will be. The heaven of the age to come will be knowing God himself, from whom all blessings flow.

Jesus himself said, "This is eternal life, that they know you the only true God, and Jesus Christ whom you have sent" (John 17:3). And Paul expressed his deepest longings like this: "I have suffered the loss of all things and count them as rubbish, in order that I may gain Christ . . . that I may know him and the power of his resurrection" (Phil. 3:8, 10). What we will enjoy most about the resurrection is having the dim mirror of this age removed and finally seeing Jesus face to face, finally knowing the triune God fully as we have been fully known by him (1 Cor. 13:12).

The resurrection from the dead is the single greatest hope of the Christian. It is the only prize that ultimately matters, and we make it our one great life goal to obtain it (Phil. 3:14). It is the culmination of the gospel (1 Pet. 3:18). The whole reason Jesus came into the world was to give us eternal life (John 3:16). He died for us, that we might live with him (1 Thess. 5:10). Jesus did not come to give us our best life now. He came to "deliver us from the present evil age" (Gal. 1:4) and "bring [us] safely into his heavenly kingdom" (2 Tim. 4:18).

Jesus is longing for this day with all his heart. He expressed this yearning to his Father when he prayed, "Father, I desire that they also, whom you have given me, may be with me where I am, to see my glory that you have given me because you loved me before the foundation of the world" (John 17:24).

Jesus's great longing is that you will be *with him*. And when you are finally with him, "he will wipe away every tear from [your] eyes, and death shall be no more, neither shall there be mourning, nor crying, nor pain anymore, for the former things [will] have passed away" (Rev. 21:4). Never again will you know any kind of separation from him (Rom. 8:39), for you "will always be with the Lord" (1 Thess. 4:17).

That is the treasure you have discovered in the field of this fallen world. Jesus has paid for it all, and it costs you everything you own in this age to have it. Yet it is such a small payment for such an everlasting, never-ending treasure that only a fool would pass it up.

The treasure makes all the difference.

Here is a call for the endurance of the saints.

REVELATION 14:12

35

DON'T GIVE UP

ALL OF US AND ENDURANCE

Various Texts

WE ALL CRAVE REST from the fatigue of living. God placed the desire for rest in our souls, and he promises to fulfill it: "I will satisfy the weary soul, and every languishing soul I will replenish" (Jer. 31:25).

In a very real way, Jesus gives rest to "all who labor and are heavy laden" and come to him (Matt. 11:28). But in this age, we cannot find complete rest.

In this age, Jesus grants us the gospel rest of ceasing the impossible labor of self-atonement for our sins (2 Cor. 5:21). But in embracing the gospel, we find ourselves also drafted into a war—a war to *keep believing* the gospel and a war to *keep spreading* it to others. In this age we "strive to enter that [complete] rest" of the age to come (Heb. 4:11).

Battles are unremitting, and wars are exhausting—especially long ones. That's why you are often tired. Many soldiers who experience the fierceness of combat want to get out of it. That's why you're tempted to escape. That's why you're tempted to give up.

But don't give up. No, rather "take courage! Do not let your hands be weak, for your work shall be rewarded" (2 Chron. 15:7).

Don't give up when that familiar sin, still crouching at your door after all these years, pounces again with temptation.

No temptation has overtaken you that is not common to man. God is faithful, and he will not let you be tempted beyond your ability, but with the temptation he will also provide the way of escape, that you may be able to endure it. (1 Cor. 10:13)

Don't give up when you feel that deep soul weariness from long battles with persistent weaknesses.

"My grace is sufficient for you, for my power is made perfect in weakness." Therefore I will boast all the more gladly of my weaknesses, so that the power of Christ may rest upon me. (2 Cor. 12:9)

Don't give up when your long asked-and-sought-and-knocked-for prayers have not yet been answered.

And he told them [the parable of the persistent widow] to the effect that they ought always to pray and not lose heart. (Luke 18:1)

Don't give up when the Devil's fiery darts of doubt find flesh and make you reel.

Therefore take up the whole armor of God, that you may be able to withstand in the evil day. . . . In all circumstances take up the shield of faith, with which you can extinguish all the flaming darts of the evil one. (Eph. 6:13, 16)

Don't give up when the fragmenting effect of multiple pressures seems relentless.

But as servants of God we commend ourselves in every way: by great endurance, in afflictions, hardships, calamities, beatings, imprisonments, riots, labors, sleepless nights, hunger . . . (2 Cor. 6:4–5)

Don't give up when the field the Lord has assigned you to is hard and the harvest does not look promising.

And let us not grow weary of doing good, for in due season we will reap, if we do not give up. (Gal. 6:9)

Don't give up when you labor in obscurity and you wonder how much it even matters.

Your Father who sees in secret will reward you. (Matt. 6:4)

Don't give up when your reputation is damaged because you are trying to be faithful to Jesus.

Blessed are you when others revile you and persecute you and utter all kinds of evil against you falsely on my account. (Matt. 5:11)

Don't give up when waiting on God seems endless.

Even youths shall faint and be weary,
　and young men shall fall exhausted;
but they who wait for the Lord shall renew their strength;
　they shall mount up with wings like eagles;
they shall run and not be weary;
　they shall walk and not faint. (Isa. 40:30–31)

Don't give up when you have failed in sin. Don't wallow. Repent (again), get your eyes off yourself (again), and fix your eyes on Jesus (again). Get up and get back in the fight.

If we confess our sins, he is faithful and just to forgive us our sins and to cleanse us from all unrighteousness. (1 John 1:9)

If we are faithless, he remains faithful—for he cannot deny himself. (2 Tim. 2:13)

Living by faith in "things not seen" is hard (Heb. 11:1). Jesus reminds us: "The way is hard that leads to life, and those who find it are [relatively] few" (Matt. 7:14). But the way has always been hard, and you are not alone in the difficulty. You are surrounded by a great cloud of witnesses who have passed this way ahead of you (Heb. 12:1). Many have suffered far more and have remained faithful. Remember them and imitate their faith (Heb. 13:7).

Above all, remember Jesus Christ (2 Tim. 2:8). Jesus knows your works (Rev. 2:2) and he understands your war (Heb. 12:3). His grace will be given to you in your time of need (Heb. 4:16), and it will be sufficient for you, even at the very worst times (2 Cor. 12:9).

So, look to Jesus (Heb. 12:2), "fight the good fight of the faith" (1 Tim. 6:12), and finish your race (2 Tim. 4:7). When you have done the will of God, you will receive what is promised: his great and eternal reward (Heb. 10:35–36). Measured by eternity, the hardships of this life will not be long, and "by your endurance you will gain your lives" (Luke 21:19).

Don't give up.

GENERAL INDEX

SCRIPTURE INDEX

"These meditations are not your ordinary exposition.
These are stories. Really good stories."
JOHN PIPER

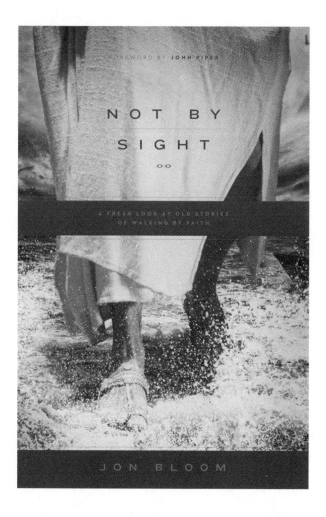

"Vivid, nourishing sketches of Bible characters learning to live with their
sometimes startling Lord."
J. I. PACKER

"Bloom's stories and insights ignite—ignite fire in bones, the old and best
paths, and glimpses of glory that make us want to run this walk of faith!"
ANN VOSKAMP

crossway.org